Leaflet.js Essentials

Create interactive, mobile-friendly mapping applications using the incredibly light yet powerful Leaflet.js platform

Paul Crickard III

PACKT PUBLISHING

open source *
community experience distilled

BIRMINGHAM - MUMBAI

Leaflet.js Essentials

Copyright © 2014 Packt Publishing

All rights reserved. No part of this book may be reproduced, stored in a retrieval system, or transmitted in any form or by any means, without the prior written permission of the publisher, except in the case of brief quotations embedded in critical articles or reviews.

Every effort has been made in the preparation of this book to ensure the accuracy of the information presented. However, the information contained in this book is sold without warranty, either express or implied. Neither the author, nor Packt Publishing, and its dealers and distributors will be held liable for any damages caused or alleged to be caused directly or indirectly by this book.

Packt Publishing has endeavored to provide trademark information about all of the companies and products mentioned in this book by the appropriate use of capitals. However, Packt Publishing cannot guarantee the accuracy of this information.

First published: August 2014

Production reference: 1110814

Published by Packt Publishing Ltd.
Livery Place
35 Livery Street
Birmingham B3 2PB, UK.

ISBN 978-1-78355-481-2

www.packtpub.com

Cover image by Pratyush Mohanta (tysoncinematics@gmail.com)

Credits

Author
Paul Crickard III

Reviewers
Drew Dara-Abrams
Akshay Joshi
Alexander Parshin
Antonio Santiago

Commissioning Editor
Pramila Balan

Acquisition Editor
Reshma Raman

Content Development Editor
Sankalp Pawar

Technical Editors
Shashank Desai
Sebastian Rodrigues

Copy Editors
Dipti Kapadia
Insiya Morbiwala
Stuti Srivastava

Project Coordinator
Harshal Ved

Proofreaders
Simran Bhogal
Maria Gould
Ameesha Green
Paul Hindle

Indexers
Mariammal Chettiyar
Rekha Nair

Production Coordinator
Nilesh R. Mohite

Cover Work
Nilesh R. Mohite

About the Author

Paul Crickard III has been programming for over 15 years and has focused on GIS and geospatial programming for 7 years. He spent 3 years working as a planner at an architecture firm, where he combined GIS with Building Information Modeling (BIM) and CAD, and built web-based GIS applications to display and modify architectural data. He has given presentations to the New Mexico Public School Facilities Authority on BIM and GIS integration and on the use of GIS for Facility Planning, and the BIM505 Users Group on GIS as an interactive frontend to BIM and editing BIM data via web applications.

Currently, Paul works as a programmer analyst in Albuquerque, specializing in the design, maintenance, and the implementation of geospatial applications. He has written plugins and extensions for ArcMap and ArcGIS Explorer Desktop to utilize NoSQL databases and send data using the Advanced Message Queuing Protocol (AMQP). Paul has built applications using OpenLayers and Leaflet.js and is currently utilizing the ESRI JavaScript API in production.

Paul tries to incorporate Python in geospatial development wherever possible. From building plugins, toolboxes, and the Field Calculator functions in ArcMap to coding standalone desktop and web applications, pyshp is his favorite library for geospatial Python applications.

When he is not coding, Paul enjoys relaxing with his wife and son, cooking, and brewing beer.

About the Reviewers

Drew Dara-Abrams is the Principal of City Building Tools, a consultancy in San Francisco (California, U.S.A.), which provides data collection and analysis services, R&D strategy and consulting, and the customized deployment of its catalog of web and mobile apps to urban designers, transportation/transit planners, and other professionals charged with the usability of office buildings, built environments, and transportation systems.

He holds a PhD in Computational Geography with an emphasis in Cognitive Science from the University of California, Santa Barbara. He previously served as the Chief Technology Officer of Kinnexxus, Inc., which builds communication devices for seniors and their families; he is also the co-founder of Strategic Spatial Solutions, Inc., which provides consulting research and development to university labs.

Dr. Dara-Abrams has also co-authored two technical textbooks: *Supporting Web Servers* and *Analyzing E-Commerce and Internet Law*, *Prentice Hall*. For more information, please visit www.citybuildingtools.com and http://drew.dara-abrams.com.

Akshay Joshi is the maintainer of the leaflet-rails Ruby gem. He has been working with web technologies for over 10 years and with mapping technologies for 5 years. Akshay is passionate about the convergence of web applications and desktop applications, and he likes to learn about the technologies that make this possible. Over the years, he has contributed to open source projects in many different languages, such as Drupal, Fog, and the Linux kernel. Currently, he is a Computer Engineering student at the University of Waterloo. When he is away from his computer, Akshay enjoys cooking for his friends and listening to new kinds of music.

Alexander Parshin is a web developer in the area of web mapping. He was the author of the first Leaflet workshop in Russia, has been the author of several Leaflet plugins, and is a contributor to the Leaflet library. His current job is related to the library as well; he is the Lead of the UI team in his company, which builds commercial B2B Web-GIS systems based on the Leaflet mapping framework.

Antonio Santiago is a Computer Science professional with more than 10 years of experience in designing and implementing systems.

Since the beginning of his professional life, his work experience has always been related to the world of meteorology; he has worked for different companies as an employee or a freelancer. He is experienced in the development of systems to collect, store, transform, analyze, and visualize data; he is also actively interested in any GIS-related technology, with preference for data visualization.

With a restless mind, which is mainly experienced in the Java ecosystem, he has also worked actively with many related web technologies and is always looking for ways to improve the client side of web applications.

A firm believer in software engineering practices, he is an enthusiast of Agile methodologies, which involves customers as the main key for the project's success.

Antonio is also the author of *OpenLayers Cookbook*, *Packt Publishing*.

www.PacktPub.com

Support files, eBooks, discount offers, and more

You might want to visit `www.PacktPub.com` for support files and downloads related to your book.

Did you know that Packt offers eBook versions of every book published, with PDF and ePub files available? You can upgrade to the eBook version at `www.PacktPub.com` and as a print book customer, you are entitled to a discount on the eBook copy. Get in touch with us at `service@packtpub.com` for more details.

At `www.PacktPub.com`, you can also read a collection of free technical articles, sign up for a range of free newsletters and receive exclusive discounts and offers on Packt books and eBooks.

PACKTLIB

`http://PacktLib.PacktPub.com`

Do you need instant solutions to your IT questions? PacktLib is Packt's online digital book library. Here, you can access, read and search across Packt's entire library of books.

Why subscribe?

- Fully searchable across every book published by Packt
- Copy and paste, print and bookmark content
- On demand and accessible via web browser

Free access for Packt account holders

If you have an account with Packt at `www.PacktPub.com`, you can use this to access PacktLib today and view nine entirely free books. Simply use your login credentials for immediate access.

I would like to dedicate this book to my wife, Yolanda. It would not have been possible without her love and support.

Table of Contents

Preface — 1
Chapter 1: Creating Maps with Leaflet — 7
  Creating a simple basemap — 8
    Referencing the JavaScript and CSS files — 8
      Using a hosted copy — 8
      Using a local copy — 9
    Creating a <div> tag to hold the map — 9
    Creating a map object — 10
    Adding a tile layer — 10
  Tile layer providers — 12
  Adding a Web Mapping Service tile layer — 15
  Multiple tile layers — 16
  Adding data to your map — 18
    Points — 19
    Polylines — 21
    Polygons — 22
  Rectangles and circles — 23
    Rectangles — 23
    Circles — 24
  MultiPolylines and MultiPolygons — 25
    MultiPolylines — 26
    MultiPolygons — 27
  Groups of layers — 28
    The layer group — 28
    Feature groups — 30
  Pop ups — 31
  Mobile mapping — 32
    HTML and CSS — 32
    Creating a mobile map with JavaScript — 34

Events and event handlers	36
Custom functions	38
Summary	**40**
Chapter 2: Mapping GeoJSON Data	**41**
Understanding the roots of GeoJSON	41
Exploring GeoJSON	42
GeoJSON in Leaflet.js	43
GeoJSON as a variable	43
Multiple geometries in GeoJSON	45
Polygons with holes	46
GeoJSON from Leaflet.js objects	48
Styling GeoJSON layers	48
Iterating through the features	50
Attaching pop ups with onEachFeature	50
Creating layers from points with pointToLayer	51
Displaying a subset of data with filter	52
Summary	**54**
Chapter 3: Creating Heatmaps and Choropleth Maps	**55**
What is a heatmap?	55
Heatmaps with Leaflet.heat	56
Using options to style your map	57
Changing the blur value	58
Changing the maxZoom value	60
Changing the radius value	60
Setting the gradient option	60
Methods of Leaflet.heat	60
Adding markers to the heatmap	61
Creating heatmaps with heatmap.js	62
Modifying the heatmap options	64
Adding more data to the map	64
Creating an interactive heatmap	65
Animating a heatmap	67
Creating a choropleth map with Leaflet	69
The GeoJSON data	70
Setting the color with a function	71
Styling the GeoJSON data	71
Creating a normalized choropleth map	73
Summary	**75**
Chapter 4: Creating Custom Markers	**77**
Creating a custom marker	77
Preparing your workspace in GIMP	78

Drawing and saving your image	79
Drawing the marker shadow	80
Using an image as an icon	81
Using a custom marker in Leaflet	**82**
Defining an L.Icon class	84
Using predefined markers with plugins	**86**
Using Mapbox Maki markers	86
Using Bootstrap and Font Awesome markers	88
Clustering markers with Leaflet.markercluster	**90**
Coding your first cluster map	90
Methods and events available to markercluster layers	93
Options that default to true	93
Other options and events	94
Animating markers with plugins	**95**
Bouncing your markers	95
Making your markers move	96
Using markers for data visualization	**100**
Using the Leaflet Data Visualization Framework plugin	100
Creating basic markers	101
Bar and pie chart markers	103
Summary	**105**
Chapter 5: ESRI in Leaflet	**107**
ESRI basemaps	**108**
Using shapefiles in Leaflet	**110**
Consuming ESRI services	**113**
Heatmaps with ESRI in Leaflet	**115**
Geocoding addresses in Leaflet	**117**
Geocoding – from an address to a point	117
Geocoding from URL parameters	119
Reverse geocoding – using points to find addresses	121
Query by attribute	**122**
Query by proximity	**124**
Summary	**126**
Chapter 6: Leaflet in Node.js, Python, and C#	**127**
Building Leaflet applications with Node.js	**128**
A basic Node.js server with Leaflet	129
Node.js, AJAX, and Leaflet	130
Node.js, Connect, and Leaflet	134
Node.js, Express, Jade, and Leaflet	136
Leaflet with Python and CherryPy	**138**
Spatial queries with Python, MongoDB, and Leaflet	142

Desktop applications in C# with Leaflet — **146**
Adding a map to a C# application — 146
Adding a marker in C# — 149
Using MongoDB with C# and Leaflet — 151
Querying with C#, Leaflet, and MongoDB — 153
Summary — **156**
Index — **157**

Preface

Making maps used to require an extensive knowledge of cartography, expensive software, and technical know-how. Today, there are numerous tools available, many of which are free, that have simplified the map-making process. This book is about using one such library, Leaflet.js.

Leaflet.js is a JavaScript library that although small, is packed with almost every feature you could need. If a feature is not available in the core library, it may be available as one of the many plugins that have become available. The largest map-making software vendor, Environmental Systems Research Institute (ESRI), has even released a plugin for Leaflet.js. If you are interested in making maps or in data visualization, Leaflet.js is the library to learn.

Whether you are looking to build simple maps or advanced mapping applications, this book will build on your JavaScript knowledge to help you reach your goal. This book was designed to be accessible to individuals who are new to map making and also to those who may know maps but are just learning to code.

What this book covers

Chapter 1, *Creating Maps with Leaflet*, walks you through the basics of making maps in Leaflet.js. You start by creating an HTML file with the minimum JavaScript code required to display a map. You are going to learn how to select different basemaps and providers and different basemap formats. Then, you will learn how to display geographic features such as points, polylines, and polygons.

Chapter 2, *Mapping GeoJSON Data*, introduces you to a geographic version of the JSON data format. You will learn how to create your own GeoJSON data as well as consume data from other sources. In this chapter, you will learn how to style the data and iterate through features to add pop ups.

Preface

Chapter 3, *Creating Heatmaps and Choropleth Maps*, moves away from simply displaying points and towards displaying the significance or comparisons of the data. It builds on what you have learned so far and teaches you how to use different plugins to create heatmaps. You will also learn how to use your knowledge of styling GeoJSON to create choropleth maps.

Chapter 4, *Creating Custom Markers*, guides you through the customization of the markers you use in your maps. You will learn how to draw your own image or modify an existing image to use it as a marker in your map. You will be introduced to several plugins that offer premade markers that are customizable. Also, you will learn how to animate markers and combine plugins for added effects.

Chapter 5, *ESRI in Leaflet*, opens up the most commonly used data formats and server endpoints in mapping. This chapter will teach you how to load shapefiles in your maps. You will also learn how to connect to an ESRI server that has an exposed REST service. Using the ESRI-Leaflet plugin, you will learn how to geocode and reverse geocode addresses, filter data from a server, and query by location.

Chapter 6, *Leaflet in Node.js, Python, and C#*, expands on everything you have learned in order to teach you how to build applications in other frameworks and languages. This chapter teaches you how to build both the frontend and the backend. You will build servers in JavaScript and Python. You will be introduced to NoSQL databases and AJAX to display and update data without refreshing your web page. Lastly, you will learn how to create a Windows desktop application by embedding Leaflet in C#.

What you need for this book

You need, at a minimum, the following software for this book:

- A web browser, preferably Google Chrome, which is available at `https://www.google.com/chrome/browser/`

For the examples in *Chapter 5*, *ESRI in Leaflet* and *Chapter 6*, *Leaflet in Node.js, Python, and C#*, the following software is required:

- Node.js, which is available at `http://nodejs.org/`.
- Python 2.7, preferably 3.x. You can download either version from `https://www.python.org/`.
- Visual Studio Express 2010. You will find a free copy at `http://www.visualstudio.com/downloads/download-visual-studio-vs`.
- CherryPy is available at `http://www.cherrypy.org/`.
- MongoDB is available at `http://www.mongodb.org/`.

- Pymongo is the Python library to use MongoDB, and it is freely available at `https://pypi.python.org/pypi/pymongo/`.
- C# drivers for MongoDB are available in several formats at `https://github.com/mongodb/mongo-csharp-driver/releases`.
- WAMP can be downloaded from `http://www.wampserver.com/en/`.

Who this book is for

If you are a map maker with some JavaScript knowledge, this book is an ideal resource that teaches you how to bring your maps to the Web and make them interactive. If you are a JavaScript developer, this book will show you how to use those skills to build powerful mapping applications.

Conventions

In this book, you will find a number of styles of text that distinguish between different kinds of information. Here are some examples of these styles, and an explanation of their meaning.

Code words in text, database table names, folder names, filenames, file extensions, pathnames, dummy URLs, user input, and Twitter handles are shown as follows: "Create a text string of the query and initialize your `StringBuilder()` method to hold the JavaScript of the function and results."

A block of code is set as follows:

```
var layer = new L.TileLayer('http://{s}.tile.thunderforest.com/
landscape/{z}/{x}/{y}.png');
map.addLayer(layer);
```

When we wish to draw your attention to a particular part of a code block, the relevant lines or items are set in bold:

```
<style>
  html, body, #map {
      padding: 0;
      margin: 0;
      height: 100%;
  }
  #points.hidden {
      display: none;
  }
</style>
```

```
<body>
<div id="map"></div>
<div id="points"></div>
```

Any command-line input or output is written as follows:

```
npm install -g connect
```

New terms and **important words** are shown in bold. Words that you see on the screen, in menus or dialog boxes for example, appear in the text like this: "You now need to right-click on the project in the **Solution Explorer** window and select **Add Reference**."

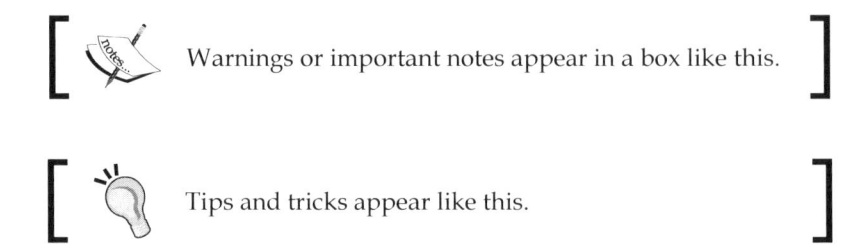

> Warnings or important notes appear in a box like this.

> Tips and tricks appear like this.

Reader feedback

Feedback from our readers is always welcome. Let us know what you think about this book—what you liked or may have disliked. Reader feedback is important for us to develop titles that you really get the most out of.

To send us general feedback, simply send an e-mail to feedback@packtpub.com, and mention the book title via the subject of your message.

If there is a topic that you have expertise in and you are interested in either writing or contributing to a book, see our author guide on www.packtpub.com/authors.

Customer support

Now that you are the proud owner of a Packt book, we have a number of things to help you to get the most from your purchase.

Downloading the example code

You can download the example code files for all Packt books you have purchased from your account at http://www.packtpub.com. If you purchased this book elsewhere, you can visit http://www.packtpub.com/support and register to have the files e-mailed directly to you.

Errata

Although we have taken every care to ensure the accuracy of our content, mistakes do happen. If you find a mistake in one of our books—maybe a mistake in the text or the code—we would be grateful if you would report this to us. By doing so, you can save other readers from frustration and help us improve subsequent versions of this book. If you find any errata, please report them by visiting http://www.packtpub.com/submit-errata, selecting your book, clicking on the **errata submission form** link, and entering the details of your errata. Once your errata are verified, your submission will be accepted and the errata will be uploaded on our website, or added to any list of existing errata, under the Errata section of that title. Any existing errata can be viewed by selecting your title from http://www.packtpub.com/support.

Piracy

Piracy of copyright material on the Internet is an ongoing problem across all media. At Packt, we take the protection of our copyright and licenses very seriously. If you come across any illegal copies of our works, in any form, on the Internet, please provide us with the location address or website name immediately so that we can pursue a remedy.

Please contact us at copyright@packtpub.com with a link to the suspected pirated material.

We appreciate your help in protecting our authors, and our ability to bring you valuable content.

Questions

You can contact us at questions@packtpub.com if you are having a problem with any aspect of the book, and we will do our best to address it.

Creating Maps with Leaflet

Web-based mapping has evolved rapidly over the last two decades, from MapQuest and Google to real-time location information on our phones' mapping apps. There have been open source projects to develop web-based maps in the past, such as MapServer, GeoServer, and OpenLayers. However, **Environmental Systems Research Institute (ESRI)** includes the Flex and Silverlight APIs; these create web-based maps from their ArcServer services.

Over the last few years, JavaScript has taken the online mapping world by storm. In 2013, there was a JS.geo conference. The library at the center of attention was Leaflet. This is a JavaScript library used to create interactive, web-based maps. With it, you can create a simple map in as little as three lines of JavaScript, or you can create complex, interactive, editable maps with hundreds of lines of code.

> You can find more information on Leaflet at `http://leafletjs.com`.

This book assumes that you have a basic understanding of HTML and CSS, primarily of how to link external `.js` and `.css` files and how to name and size a `<div>` element. It also assumes that you have a working knowledge of JavaScript.

In this chapter, we will cover the following topics:

- Tile layers
- Vector layers
- Pop ups
- Custom functions / Responding to events
- Mobile mapping

Creating a simple basemap

To create a map with Leaflet, you need to do the following four things:

- Reference the JavaScript and **Cascading Style Sheet** (**CSS**) files
- Create a `<div>` element to hold the map
- Create a `map` object
- Add a tile layer (base layer)

Before we get into the details of building the map, let's set up an HTML file that we can use throughout the book. Open a text editor and enter the following HTML:

```
<!DOCTYPE html><html>
<head><title>Leaflet Essentials</title>
</head>
<body>
</body>
</html>
```

Save the file as `LeafletEssentials.html`. We will add to this file throughout the rest of the book.

> **Downloading the example code**
>
> You can download the example code files for all Packt books you have purchased from your account at `http://www.packtpub.com`. If you purchased this book elsewhere, you can visit `http://www.packtpub.com/support` and register to have the files e-mailed directly to you.

Referencing the JavaScript and CSS files

There are two ways to load Leaflet into your code: you can either reference a hosted file or download a copy to your local machine and reference that copy. The next two sections will cover how you can set up your environment for a hosted copy or for a local copy.

Using a hosted copy

We will not be making any changes to the original CSS or JS files, so we will link to the hosted version.

In a text editor, open `LeafletEssentials.html`. In the `<head>` element, and after the `</title>` element, add the following code:

```
<link rel="stylesheet" href="http://cdn.leafletjs.com/leaflet-
0.7.3/leaflet.css"0.7.3 />
```

[8]

After the `<body>` tag, add the following code:

```
<script src="http://cdn.leafletjs.com/leaflet-
0.7.3/Leaflet"></script>
```

The links are standard HTML for `<link>` and `<script>`. Open either link in your browser and you will see the contents of the files.

Using a local copy

Using a local copy is the same as a hosted copy, except the path to the files is different. Download `Leaflet.js` from http://leafletjs.com/download.html and extract it to your desktop. If you downloaded `Leaflet-0.7.3.zip`, you should have a folder with the same name. In the folder, you will find a subfolder named `images` and the following three files:

- `Leaflet.css`: This is the cascading style sheet
- `Leaflet`: This is a compressed version of Leaflet
- `Leaflet-src.js`: This is the full version of Leaflet for developers

Add the following code in the `<head>` tag of `LeafletEssentials.html`:

```
<link rel="stylesheet"href="\PATH TO DESKTOP\leaflet-
0.7.3\leaflet.css" />
```

Add the following code in the `<body>` tag of `LeafletEssentials.html`:

```
<script src="\leaflet-0.7.3\Leaflet"></script>0.7.3Leaflet
```

You now have local references to the Leaflet library and CSS. We are using the `Leaflet` file because it is smaller and will load faster. As long as you do not need to add any code to the file, you can delete the `Leaflet-src.js` file.

Creating a <div> tag to hold the map

You need a place to put the map. You can accomplished this by creating a `<div>` tag with an ID that will be referenced by a `map` object. The `<div>` tag that is holding the map needs a defined height. The easiest way to give the tag a height is to use CSS in the `<div>` tag that you created. Add the following code to the `<body>` tag of `LeafletEssentials.html` after the `<script>` reference to the `Leaflet` file:

```
<div id="map" style="width: 600px; height: 400px"></div>
```

> Style the `<div>` tag in the HTML file and *not* the `Leaflet.css` file. If you do this, the map `<div>` size will be global for every page that uses it.

[9]

Creating a map object

Now that you have the references and a place to put the map, it is time to start coding the map using JavaScript. The first step is to create a `map` object. The `map` class takes a `<div>` tag (which you created in the previous step) and `options`: `L.map(div id, options)`. To create a map object named `map`, add the following code after the `<script>` element in `LeafletEssentials.html`:

```
var map = L.map('map',{center: [35.10418, -106.62987],
zoom: 10
});
```

Alternatively, you can shorten the code using the `setView()` method, which takes the `center` and `zoom` options as parameters:

```
var map = L.map('map').setView([35.10418, -106.62987],10);
```

In the preceding code, you created a new instance of the `map` class and named it `map`. You may be used to creating new instances of a class using the keyword `new`; this is shown in the following code:

```
var map = new L.Map();
```

Leaflet implements factories that remove the need for the `new` keyword. In this example, `L.map()` has been given the `<div>` map and two options: `center` and `zoom`. These two options position the map on the screen with the latitude and longitude in the center of the `<div>` element and zoomed in or out at the desired level. The `center` option takes the `[latitude, longitude]` parameters, and `zoom` takes an integer; the larger the number, the tighter the zoom.

> It is good practice to always assign the `center` and `zoom` options. There is nothing worse than seeing a map of the world when all of the data is located Albuquerque, NM.

Adding a tile layer

The last step to create your first map in Leaflet is to add a tile layer. A tile layer can be thought of as your basemap. It is the imagery that you will add points, lines, and polygons on top of later in the book. Tile layers are a service provided by a tile server. A tile server usually breaks up the layer into 256 x 256 pixel images. You retrieve the images needed based on your location and zoom through a URL that requests `/z/x/y.png`. Only these tiles are loaded. As you pan and zoom, new tiles are added to your map.

Chapter 1

The tile layer, at a minimum, requires the URL to a tile server. In this book, we will use OpenStreetMap for our tile layer.

> You need to abide by the terms of service to use OpenStreetMap tiles. The TOS is available at http://wiki.openstreetmap.org/wiki/Tile_usage_policy.

The URL to the OpenStreetMap tile server is shown in the following code:

```
L.tileLayer('http://{s}.tile.osm.org/{z}/{x}/{y}.png').addTo(map);
```

In the code, we provide the URL template to OpenStreetMaps. We also call the addTo() method so that the layer is drawn. We need to pass L.map() as a parameter to the addTo() function. We named our L.map() instance map in the previous section (var map = L.map()).

> Leaflet allows method chaining: the calling of multiple methods on an object at the same time. This is what we did when we put .addTo(map) at the end of the line, creating the instance of L.tileLayer(). The longer way of adding the layer to the map without chaining is to assign the instance to a variable and then call addTo() from the variable, as shown in the following code:
> ```
> var x = L.tileLayer('http://{s}.tile.osm.org/{z}/{x}/{y}.png');
> x.addTo(map);
> ```

You now have a complete map that allows you to pan and zoom around the world. Your LeafletEssentials.html file should look like the following code:

```
<html>
<head><title>Leaflet Essentials</title>
<link rel="stylesheet" href="http://cdn.leafletjs.com/leaflet-0.7.3/leaflet.css" />
</head>
<body>
<script src="http://cdn.leafletjs.com/leaflet-0.7.3/Leaflet"></script>
<div id="map" style="width: 600px; height: 400px"></div>
<script>
var map = L.map('map',
{
```

[11]

```
    center: [35.10418, -106.62987],
    zoom: 10
});
L.tileLayer('http://{s}.tile.osm.org/{z}/{x}/{y}.png').addTo(map);
</script>
</body>
</html>
```

Even with liberal spacing, you were able to build a fully functional map of the world with pan and zoom capabilities in six lines of JavaScript. The following screenshot shows the finished map:

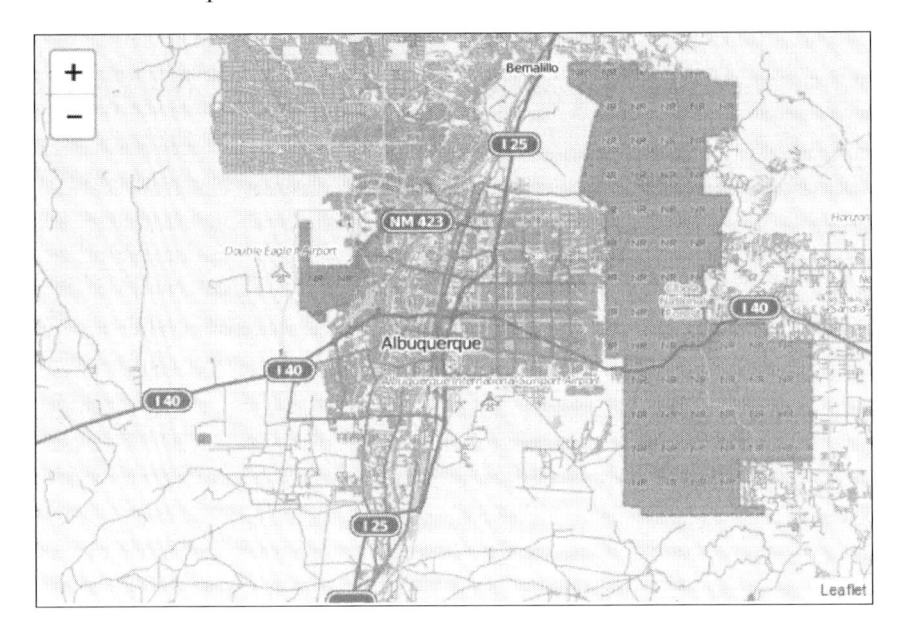

Tile layer providers

Now that you have created your first map, you are probably wondering how to change the tile layer to something else. There are several tile layer providers, some of which require registration. This section will present you with two more options: Thunderforest and Stamen. Thunderforest provides tiles that extend OpenStreetMap, while Stamen provides more artistic map tiles. Both of these services can be used to add a different style of basemap to your Leaflet map.

Thunderforest provides five tile services:

- OpenCycleMap
- Transport

- Landscape
- Outdoors
- Atlas (still in development)

To use Thunderforest, you need to point your tile layer to the URL of the tile server. The following code shows how you can add a Thunderforest tile layer:

```
var layer = new L.TileLayer('http://{s}.tile.thunderforest.com/
landscape/{z}/{x}/{y}.png');
map.addLayer(layer);
```

The preceding code loads the landscape tile layer. To use another layer, just replace `landscape` in the URL with `cycle`, `transport`, or `outdoors`. The following screenshot shows the Thunderforest landscape layer loaded in Leaflet:

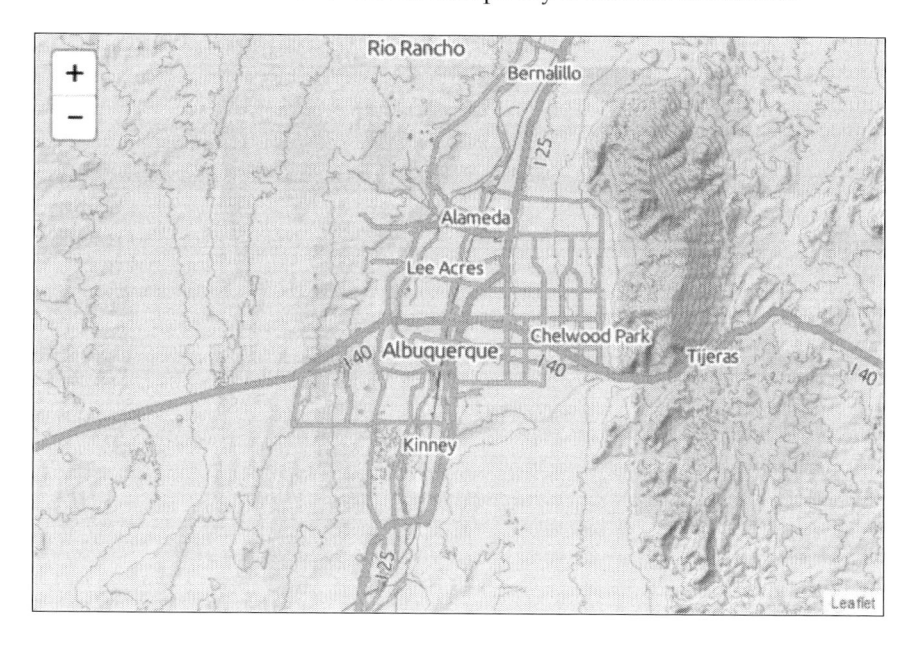

Stamen provides six tile layers; however, we will only discuss the following three layers:

- Terrain (available in the United States only)
- Watercolor
- Toner

The other three are Burning Map, Mars and Trees, and Cabs & Crime. The Burning Map and Mars layers require WebGL, and Trees and Cabs & Crime are only available in San Francisco. While these maps have a definite wow factor, they are not practical for our purposes here.

Creating Maps with Leaflet

> Learn about the Stamen tile layers, including Burning Map, Mars and Trees, and Cabs & Crime, at http://maps.stamen.com.

Stamen requires you to follow the same steps as Thunderforest, but it includes an additional step of adding a reference to the JavaScript file. After the reference to your Leaflet file, add the following reference:

```
<script type="text/javascript"
src="http://maps.stamen.com/js/tile.stamen.js?v1.2.4"></script>
```

Instead of `L.TileLayer()`, Stamen uses `L.StamenTileLayer(tile set name)`. Replace the tile set name with `terrain`, `watercolor`, or `toner`. Lastly, add `addLayer()` to the map as shown in the following code:

```
var layer = new L.StamenTileLayer("watercolor");
map.addLayer(layer);
```

Stamen's tile layers are not your typical basemap layers; they are works of cartographic art.

> Stamen has an online tool to edit map layers and save the output as an image. To create your own artistic map images, go to http://mapstack.stamen.com.

The following screenshot shows the Stamen watercolor layer loaded in Leaflet. As you zoom in, you will see more detail:

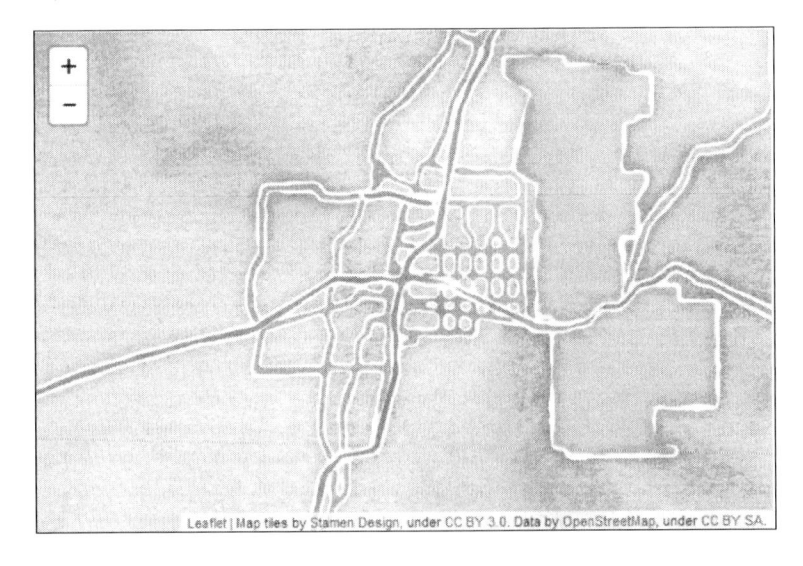

[14]

Adding a Web Mapping Service tile layer

Another type of tile layer that can be added to a Leaflet map is a **Web Mapping Service** (**WMS**) tile layer. WMS is a way to request and transfer map images over the Web through HTTP. It is an **Open Geospatial Consortium** (**OGC**) specification.

> For detailed technical information on the WMS specification, see the OGC website: `http://www.opengeospatial.org/standards/wms`.

With an understanding of how to add tile layers, and having seen several examples, you may have noticed that none of the examples were of satellite imagery. The first WMS layer you will add to your map is the **United States Geological Survey** (**USGS**) Imagery Topo.

Like the `L.tileLayer()` function that we used previously, the `L.tileLayer.wms()` function takes a URL and a set of options as parameters. The following code adds the WMS layer to your map:

```
varusgs =
L.tileLayer.wms("http://basemap.nationalmap.gov/ArcGIS/services/USGSImageryTopo/MapServer/WMSServer", {
layers:'0',
format: 'image/png',
transparent: true,
attribution: "USGS"
}).addTo(map);
```

The URL for the WMS was taken from the USGS website. You can find other WMS layers at `http://basemap.nationalmap.gov/arcgis/rest/services`. The options specified are the layer name, the format, the transparency, and the attribution. The layer name will be provided on the information page of the service you are connecting to. The format is an image, and the transparency is set to `true`. Since this layer covers the globe, and we are not putting any other layers underneath it, the transparency could be set to `false`. In the next example, you will see how setting the transparency to `true` allows another layer to become visible. Lastly, there is an attribution set to USGS. When you assign an attribution to a layer, Leaflet adds the text value in the lower-right corner of the map. It is important to use an attribution as it is similar to citing a source in text. If it is not your data, it is accepted practice to give credit where credit is due. Many times, it is also required by copyright. Since this layer is from the USGS, it is accredited in the attribution property of the layer.

Creating Maps with Leaflet

> The attribution value can contain hyperlinks, as shown in the following code:
> ```
> attribution: "<a
> href='http://basemap.nationalmap.gov/arcgis/rest/
> service
> s'>USGS</a>"
> ```

Insert the WMS layer code into `LeafletEssentials.html`, and you should now have a map with satellite imagery. The following screenshot shows the satellite imagery loaded into Leaflet:

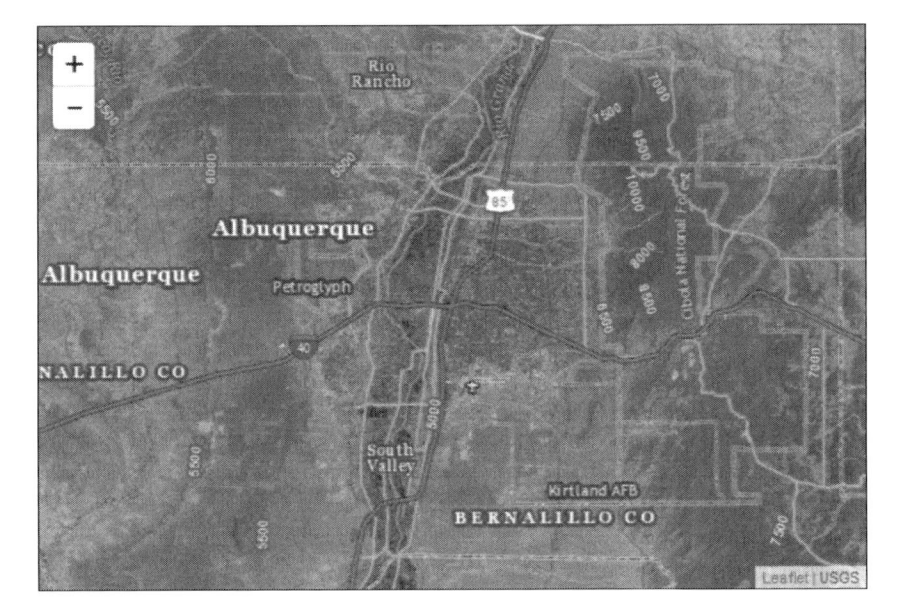

Multiple tile layers

In the previous example, you added a WMS layer and set the transparency to `true`. The reason you need to do this is because you can add multiple tile layers on top of each other, and with the transparency set to `true`, you will be able to see them all at the same time. In this example, you need to add the **National Weather Service** (**NWS**) radar mosaic WMS on top of the USGS satellite imagery.

> The **National Oceanic and Atmospheric Administration (NOAA)** provides a list of several WMS layers; they are available at the following link:
>
> http://nowcoast.noaa.gov/help/mapservices.shtml?name=mapservices

The adding of extra WMS layers follows the same format as the previous example, but with a different URL, layer name, and attribution. Add the following code after the code for the satellite imagery in `LeafletEssentials.html`:

```
Varnexrad = 
L.tileLayer.wms("http://nowcoast.noaa.gov/wms/com.esri.wms.Esrimap
/obs", {
layers: 'RAS_RIDGE_NEXRAD',
format: 'image/png',
transparent: true,
attribution: "NOAA/NWS"
}).addTo(map);
```

This code adds the NOAA WMS layer for the NWS radar mosaic. Note that the URL and layer have changed and the attribution is set to NOAA/NWS. The RAS_RIDGE_NEXRAD layer is a grid that displays values when they begin to exist. The name of the layer can be found on the NOAA website; you are not expected to remember that RAS_RIDGE_NEXRAD is the weather radar layer. There are large portions of the map with no data, and since we set the transparency to true, these blank spaces allow the satellite imagery to become visible. Your map should now show the satellite imagery with the radar mosaic overlaid, as in the following screenshot:

Creating Maps with Leaflet

If you set the transparency to `false`, you allow the layer to draw on the entire map. Areas with no data are displayed as white squares and cover the satellite imagery underneath, as shown in the following screenshot:

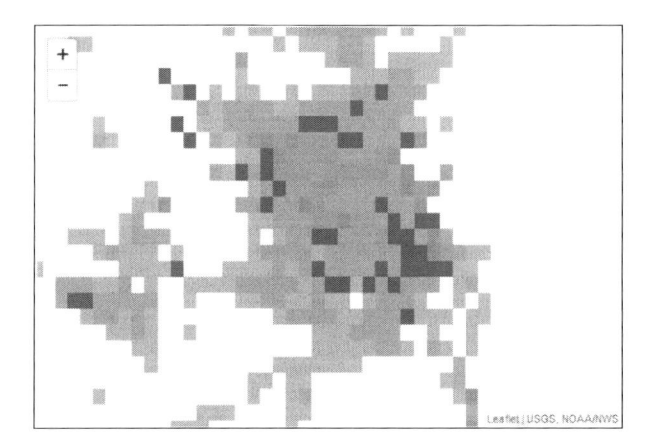

WMS layers do not need to serve as base layers only; they can be used as additional data. This was shown in the previous example where you overlaid the radar on the satellite imagery. In this example, you used a satellite image. You can also use the OpenStreetMap tile layer from the first map. Again, just set the transparency to `true`. WMS layers can be added just like points, lines, and polygons, which is discussed in the following sections.

Adding data to your map

So far, you have learned how to add tile layers to a map. In the previous example, you added a WMS layer on top of a base tile layer. Now, you will learn how to draw your own layers that need to be added on top of a tile layer. The three geometric primitives of vector data that you can add to a map are often referred to as points, lines, and polygons.

In this section, you will learn how to add markers, polylines, and polygons to your map.

Points

So far, your map is not that interesting. You often draw a map to highlight a specific place or point. Leaflet has a `Point` class; however, it is not used to simply add a point on the map with an icon to specify the place. In Leaflet, points are added to the map using the `Marker` class. At minimum, the `Marker` class requires a latitude and longitude, as shown in the following code:

```
Var myMarker = L.marker([35.10418, -106.62987]).addTo(map);
```

> You can create a marker by simply calling `L.marker([lat,long]).addTo(map);`, but assigning the marker to a variable will allow you to interact with it by name. How do you delete a specific marker if it does not have a name?

In the preceding code, you created a marker at point [35.10418, -106.62987], and then, as with the tile layer, you used the `addTo(map)` function. This created a marker icon at the specified latitude and longitude. The following screenshot shows the marker on the map:

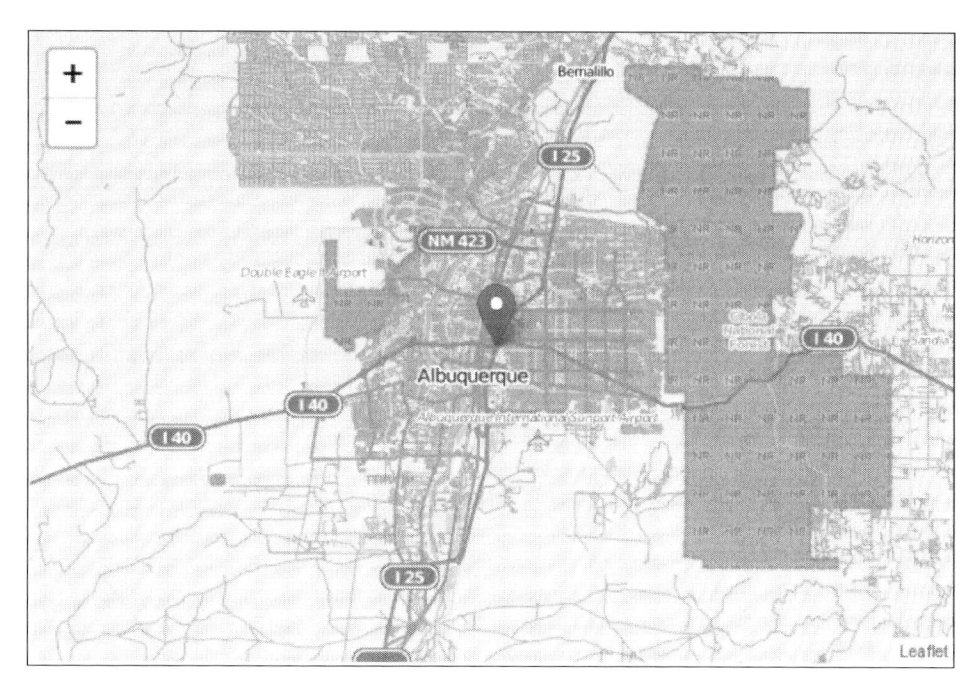

The preceding example is a simplified, and almost useless, marker. The `Marker` class has options, events, and methods that you can call to make them more interactive and useful. You will learn about methods—specifically the `bindPopup()` method—and events later in this chapter.

There are 10 options you can specify when creating a marker, as follows:

- `icon`
- `clickable`
- `draggable`
- `keyboard`
- `title`
- `alt`
- `zIndexOffset`
- `opacity`
- `riseOnHover`
- `riseOffset`

The options `clickable`, `draggable`, `keyboard`, `zIndexOffset`, `opacity`, `riseOnHover`, and `riseOffset` are all set to a default value. In *Chapter 4, Creating Custom Markers*, you will learn about the `icon` option in detail. Two options that you should set are `title` and `alt`. The `title` option is the tooltip text that will be displayed when you hover over the point with the cursor, and the `alt` option is the alternative text that is read using screen readers for accessibility. These options are used in the following code:

```
varmyMarker = L.marker([35.10418, -106.62987],
{title:"MyPoint",alt:"The Big I",draggable:true}).addTo(map);
```

The code extends the original marker example by adding a title and alt text and making the marker draggable. You will use the `draggable` options with an event in the last section of this chapter. The options are set the same as when we created our map instance; use curly braces to group the options, and separate each option with a comma. This is how options will be set for all objects.

Polylines

The first vector layer you will learn to create is aLine. In Leaflet, you will use the `Polyline` class. A polyline can represent a single line segment or a line with multiple segments. Polylines and polygons extend the `path` class. You do not call `path` directly, but you have access to its methods, properties, and events. To draw a polyline, you need to provide at least a single longitude and latitude pair. The option for a polyline is set as default, so you need not specify any values unless you want to override the default. This is shown in the following code:

```
var polyline = L.polyline([[35.10418, -106.62987],[35.19738, -106.875]], {color: 'red',weight:8}).addTo(map);
```

In this example, the polyline is `red` and has a weight of `8`. The `weight` option defaults to `5`. If you want a thicker line, increase the number. For a thinner line, decrease the number. To add more segments to the line, just add additional latitude and longitude values as shown in the following code:

```
var polyline = L.polyline([[35.10418, -106.62987],[35.19738, -106.875],[35.07946, -106.80634]], {color: 'red',weight:8}).addTo(map);
```

> You need to first provide a latitude and longitude pair because a line consists of at least two points. Afterwards, you can declare additional latitudes and longitudes to extend your line.

The following screenshot shows the polyline added to the map:

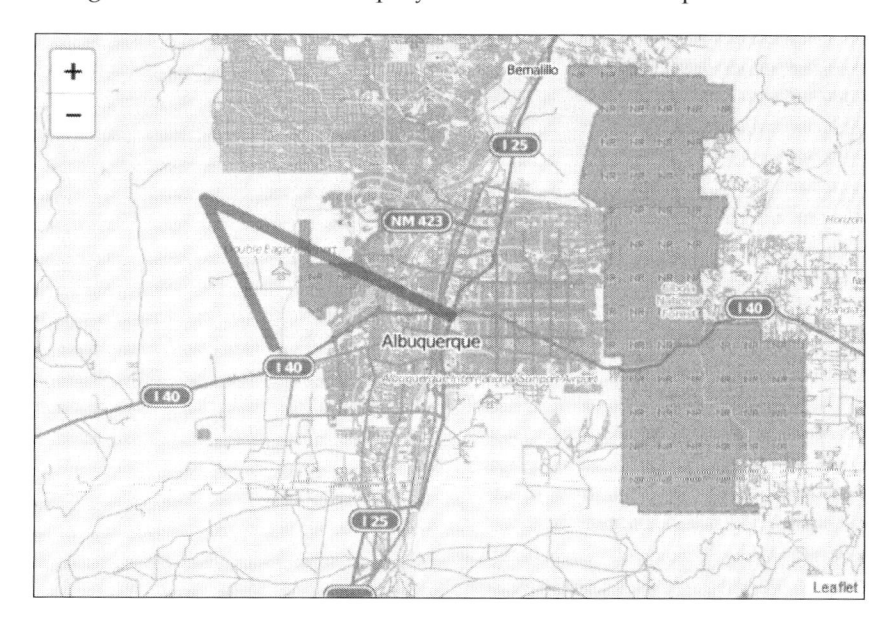

Polygons

A polygon is a polyline that is closed. Polygons tend to be classified by the number of sides, as follows:

- Triangle (3)
- Hexagon (6)
- Octagon (8)

Leaflet has a class for drawing two common polygons: a circle and a rectangle. When drawing a polygon, you will specify a minimum of three coordinates. A triangle is the simplest polygon that you can draw. That is why you need to provide at least three points. You do not need to specify the starting point at the end of the list. Leaflet will automatically close the polygon for you. To draw a polygon, simply copy the code for the polyline with three points and change the class to `L.polygon()`, as shown in the following code:

```
var polygon = L.polygon([[35.10418, -106.62987],[35.19738, -106.875],[35.07946, -106.80634]], {color: 'red',weight:8}).addTo(map);
```

Since Leaflet automatically closes the polygon, our three-point polyline can become a polygon. Since `polyline` and `polygon` inherit from `path`, the options `color` and `weight` apply to both. You will notice that `color` and `weight` refer to the outline of the polygon. Two options that you will find useful when drawing polygons are `fillColor` and `fillOpacity`:

```
var polygon = L.polygon([[35.10418, -106.62987],[35.19738, -106.875],[35.07946, -106.80634]], {color: 'red',weight:8,fillColor:'blue',fillOpacity:1}).addTo(map);
```

The preceding code draws a `red` triangle with a weight of 8. The additional options of `fillColor` and `fillOpacity` are set to `blue` and 1. The fill color of a polygon will be set to the default if no `fillColor` option is selected. You only need to use `fillColor` if you want a different fill color than the outline.

> Opacity is a value between 0 and 1, where 0 is 100 percent opacity and 1 is no opacity (solid).

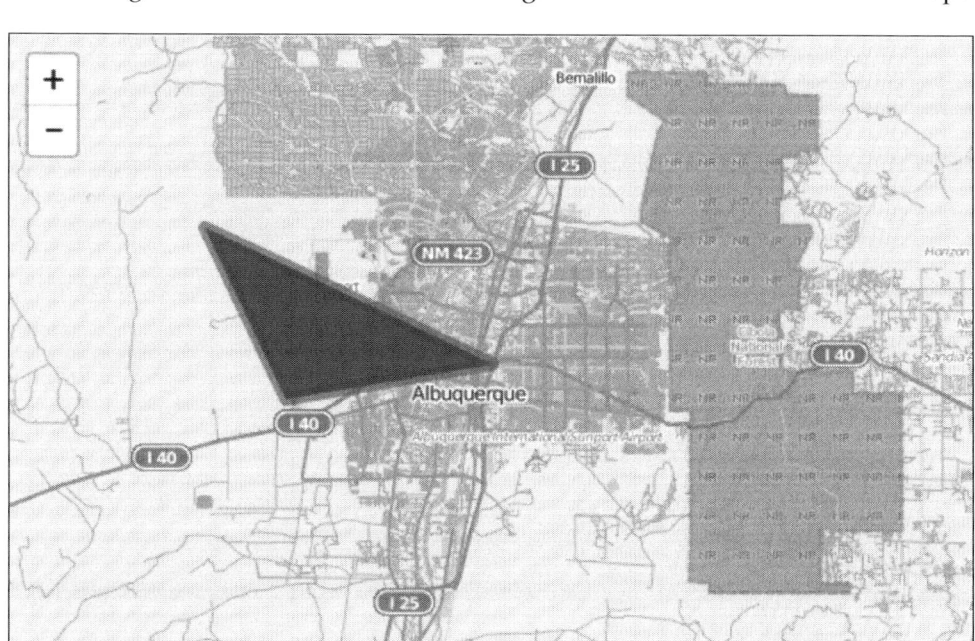

The following screenshot shows the red triangle with a blue fill added to the map:

Rectangles and circles

Circles and rectangles are common polygons that have built-in classes in Leaflet. You can also draw them manually using polygon and by specifying all of the line segments, but that would be a difficult route to take.

Rectangles

To create a rectangle, you need an instance of the class `L.rectangle()` with the latitude and longitude pair for the upper-left corner and lower-right corner as a parameter. The class extends `L.polygon()`, so you have access to the same options, methods, and events:

```
var myRectangle = L.rectangle([[35.19738, -106.875],[35.10418, -106.62987]], {color: "red", weight: 8,fillColor:"blue"}).addTo(map);
```

Creating Maps with Leaflet

The preceding code uses the first two points in the polyline and triangle, but in reverse order (upper left and lower right). The options are the same as the polygon, but with opacity removed. The following screenshot shows the rectangle added to the map:

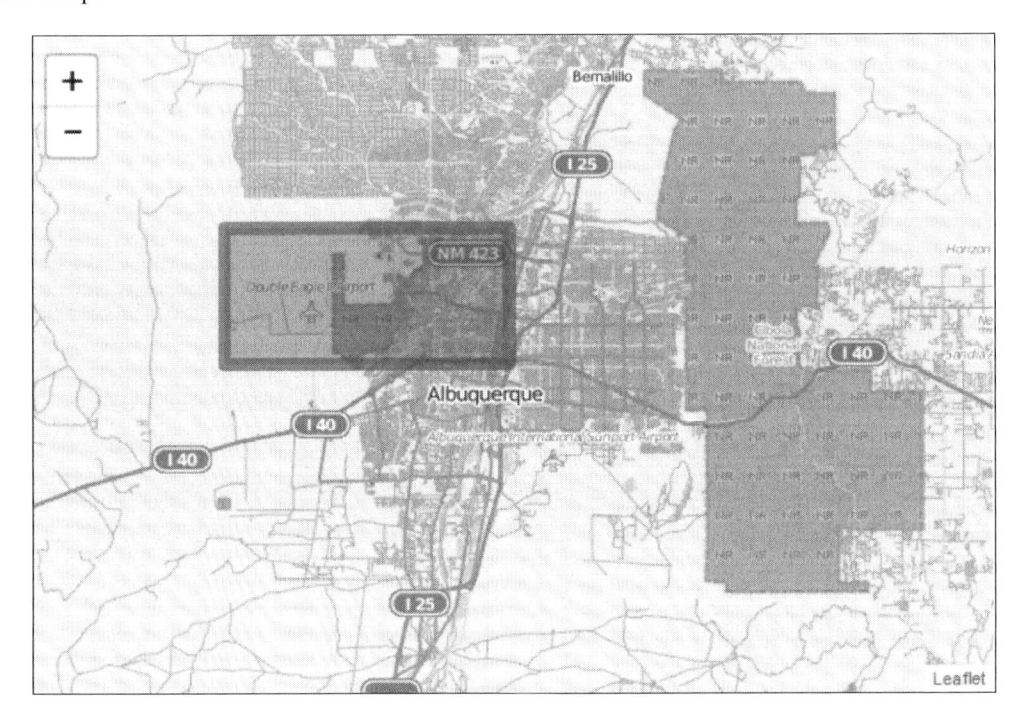

Circles

To create a circle, you need an instance of `L.circle()` with the center point and a radius (in meters) as parameters. You can specify the same options as you used in your rectangle because the `circle` class extends the `path` class. This is shown in the following code:

```
L.circle([35.10418, -106.62987], 8046.72,{color: "red", weight:
8,fillColor:"blue"}).addTo(map);
```

Chapter 1

The preceding code specifies the center point, a radius of 5 miles (8046.72 meters), and the same options as the rectangle in the previous example. The following screenshot shows the circle added to the map:

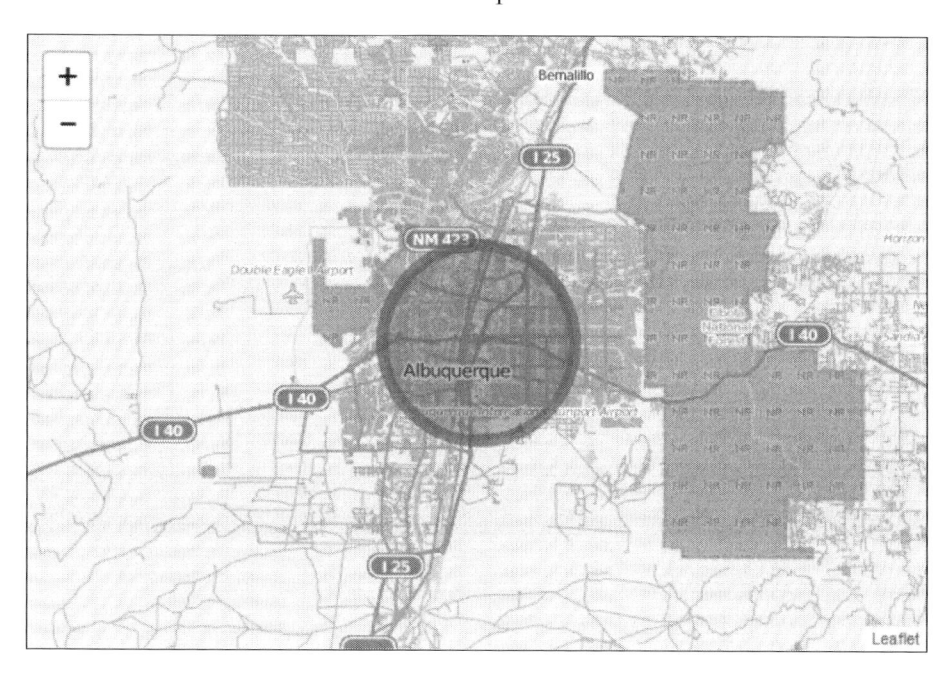

MultiPolylines and MultiPolygons

In the previous examples, you created each polyline and polygon as its own layer. When you start creating real data, you will find that you want multiple polylines or polygons on a single layer. For starters, it is more realistic, and it also makes it possible to deal with similar features as a single entity. If you want to map parks and bike trails on a single map, it makes sense to add the parks as MultiPolygon and the bike trails as MultiPolyline. Then, you can provide the user with the option of turning either layer on or off.

> Bracketing for MultiPolylines and MultiPolygons can get confusing. You need brackets to hold the MultiPolyline or MultiPolygon, brackets for each polyline or polygon, and brackets for each latitude and longitude.

[25]

MultiPolylines

Creating a MultiPolyline is functionally the same as a single polyline, except that you pass multiple longitudes and latitudes; a set for each polygon. This is shown in the following code:

```
var multipolyline = L.multiPolyline([[[35.10418,-
106.62987],[35.19738,-106.875],[35.07946,-
106.80634]],[[35.11654,-106.58318],[35.13142,-
106.48876],[35.07384,-106.52412]]],{color:
'red',weight:8}).addTo(map);
```

In the preceding code, the first polyline is the same as the polyline example. A second polyline is added, and the options are also the same as the first polyline example. The following screenshot shows the MultiPolyline added to the map:

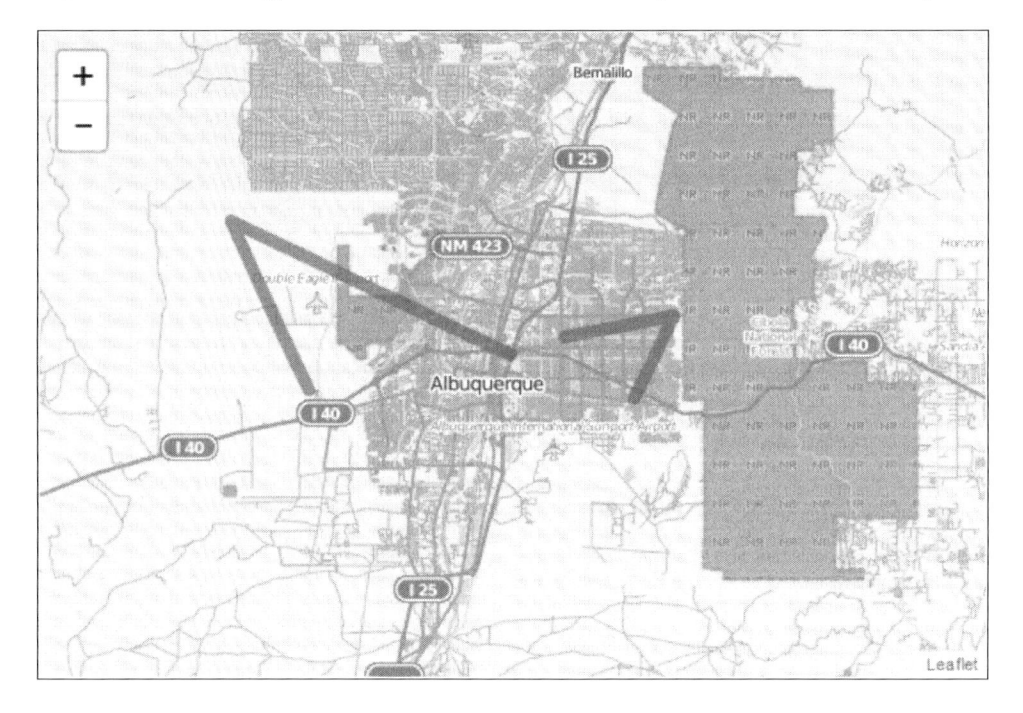

MultiPolygons

Creating a MultiPolygon is the same as creating a MultiPolyline. Since Leaflet will automatically close the polyline, as long as our polylines have three or more points, we can use them. This is shown in the following code:

```
var multipolygon = L.multiPolygon([[[35.10418,-
106.62987],[35.19738,-106.875],[35.07946,-
106.80634]],[[35.11654,-106.58318],[35.13142,-
106.48876],[35.07384,-106.52412]]],{color:
'red',weight:8}).addTo(map).bindPopup("We are the same layer");
```

In the preceding code, you can see that the parameters used are identical to those used in the MultiPolyline example earlier. When we create a MultiPolygon or MultiPolyline, the options will apply to every polygon or polyline in the collection. This means that they all have to be the same color, weight, opacity, and so on. There is a new method in the preceding code: `.bindPopup("We are the same layer")`. MultiPolygons and MultiPolylines also share the same pop up. Pop ups will be discussed later in this chapter. Also, note the use of method chaining in the line `L.multiPolygon().addTo().bindPopup()`. The following screenshot shows the MultiPolygon added to the map:

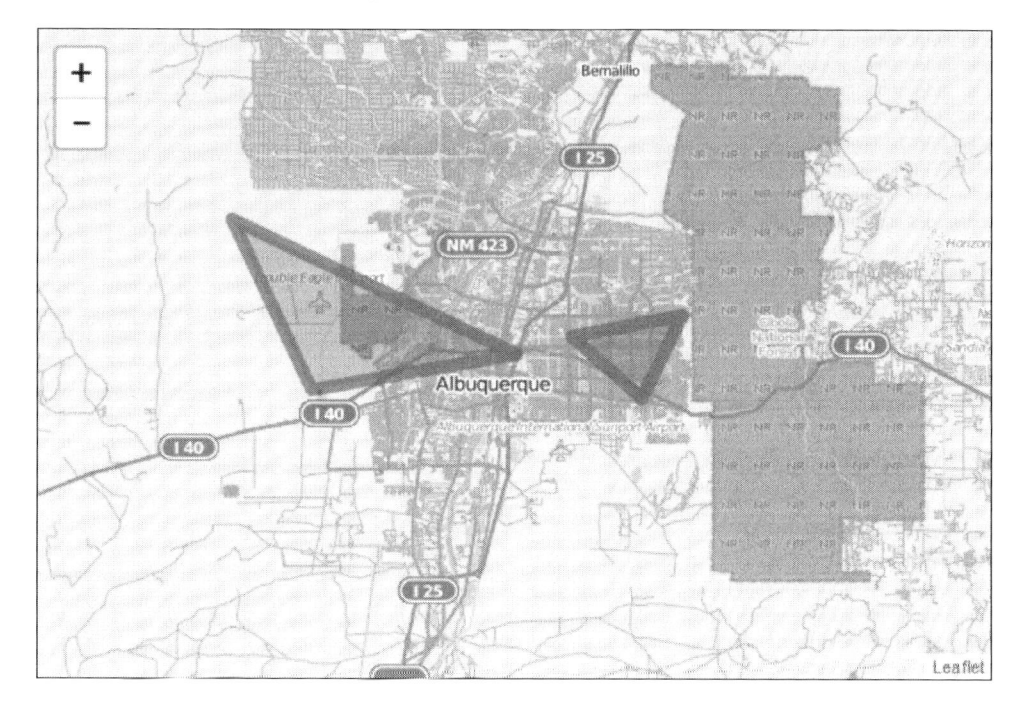

Groups of layers

MultiPolyline and MultiPolygon layers allow you to combine multiple polylines and polygons. If you want to create group layers of different types, such as a marker layer with a circle, you can use a layer group or a feature group.

The layer group

A layer group allows you to add multiple layers of different types to the map and manage them as a single layer. To use a layer group, you will need to define several layers:

```
var marker=L.marker([35.10418, -106.62987]).bindPopup("I am a Marker");
var marker2=L.marker([35.02381, -106.63811]).bindPopup("I am Marker 2");
var polyline=L.polyline([[35.10418, -106.62987],[35.19738, -106.875],[35.07946, -106.80634]], {color: 'red',weight:8}).bindPopup("I am a Polyline");
```

The preceding code creates two markers and a polyline. Note that you will not use the `addTo(map)` function after creating the layers, like you did in the previous examples. You will let the layer group handle adding the layer to the map. A layer group requires a set of layers as a parameter:

```
var myLayerGroup=L.layerGroup([marker, polyline]).addTo(map);
```

In the previous code, an instance of `L.layerGroup()` was created as `myLayerGroup`. The layers passed as a parameter were `marker` and `polyline`. Finally, the layer group was added to the map. The earlier code shows three layers, but only two were added to the layer group. To add layers to a layer group without passing them as a parameter during creation, you can use the layer group `addLayer()` method. This method takes a layer as a parameter, as shown in the following code:

```
myLayerGroup.addLayer(marker2);
```

Now, all three layers have been added to the layer group and are displayed on the map. The following screenshot shows the layer group added to the map:

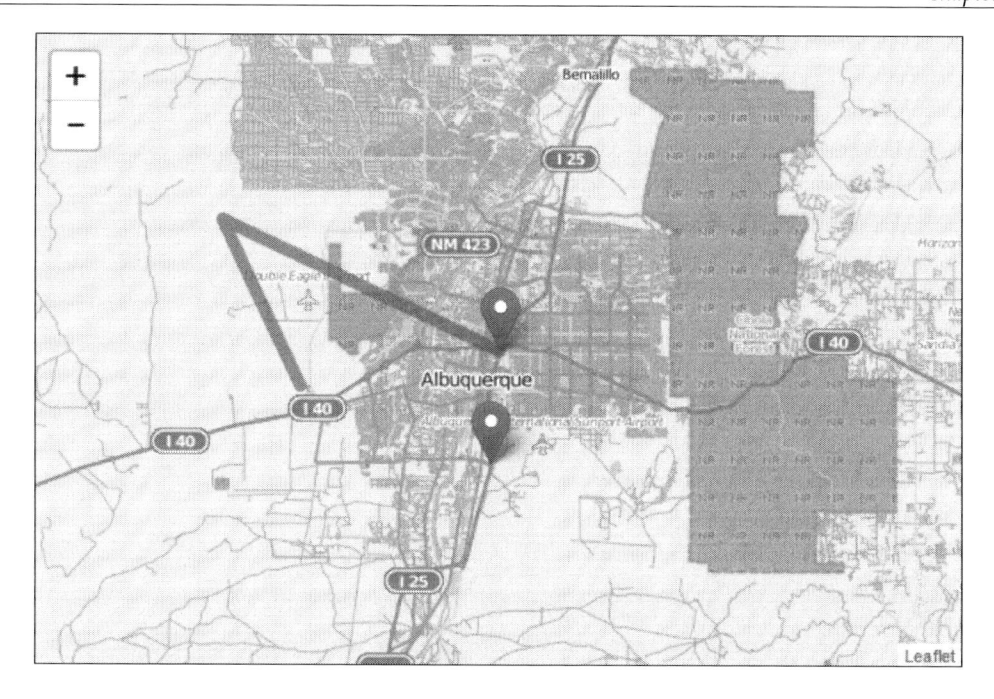

If you want to remove a layer from the layer group, you can use the `removeLayer()` method and pass the layer name as a parameter:

```
myLayerGroup.removeLayer(marker);
```

If you remove a layer from the group, it will no longer be displayed on the map because the `addTo()` function was called for the layer group and not the individual layer. If you want to display the layer but no longer want it to be part of the layer group, use the `removeLayer()` function, as shown in the preceding code, and then add the layer to the map as shown in the earlier examples. This is shown in the following code:

```
marker.addTo(map);
```

All style options and pop ups need to be assigned to the layer when it is created. You cannot assign a style or pop ups to a layer group as a whole. This is where feature groups can be used.

Feature groups

A feature group is similar to a layer group, but extends it to allow mouse events and includes the `bindPopup()` method. The constructor for a feature group is the same as the layer group: just pass a set of layers as a parameter. The following code displays an example of a feature group:

```
VarmyfeatureGroup=L.featureGroup([marker, marker2, polyline])
    .addTo(map).setStyle({color:'purple',opacity:.5})
    .bindPopup("We have the same popup because we are a group");
```

In the preceding code, the layers added are the same three that you added in the layer group. Since the feature group extends the layer group, you can assign a style and pop up to all of the layers at once. The following screenshot shows the feature group added to the map:

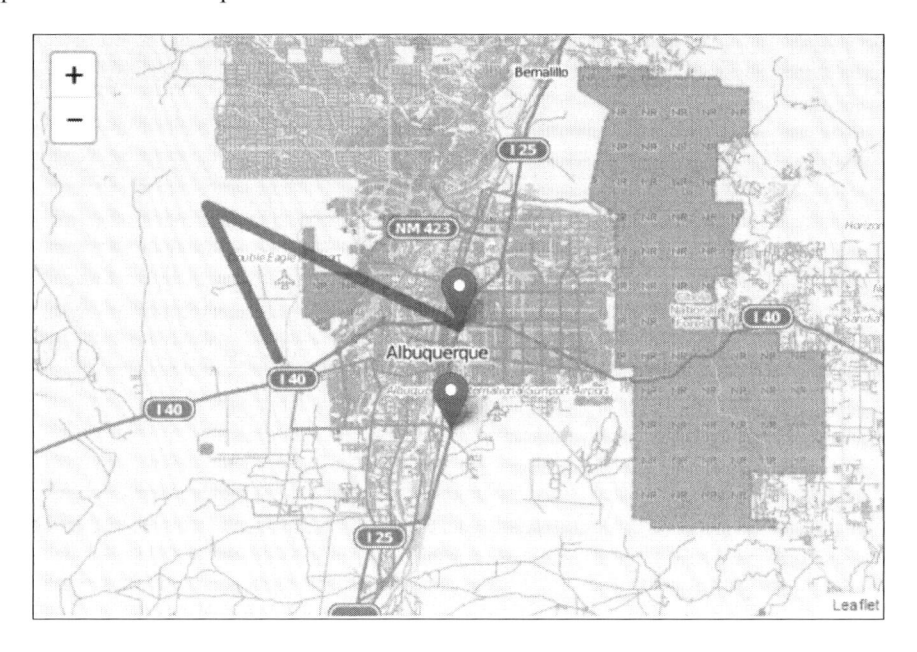

When you created the polyline in the previous example, you set the color to `red`. Note now that since you passed style information to the feature group by setting the color to `purple`, the polyline took the information from the feature group and discarded its original settings. If you removed the polyline from the feature group, it will be removed from the map as well. If you try to add the polyline to the map using `addTo()`, as in the previous examples, it will still be purple and have the new pop up. The markers are still blue even though you passed style information to the feature group. The `setStyle()` method only applies to layers in the feature group that have a `setStyle()` method. Since a polyline extends the `path` class, it has a `setStyle()` method. The markers do not have a `setStyle()` method, so their color did not change.

Pop ups

The last few examples introduced pop ups. A pop up provides a way to make your layers interactive or provides information to the user. The simplest way to add a pop up to a marker, polyline, or polygon is to use the `bindPopup()` method. This method takes the contents of the pop up as a parameter. Using the `marker` variable we created earlier, we bind the pop up to it with the following code:

```
marker.bindPopup("I am a marker");
```

The `bindPopup()` method allows you to enter HTML as the content. This is shown in the following code:

```
marker.bindPopup("<h1>My Marker</h1><p>This is information about
the marker</p><ul><li>Info 1</li><li>Info 2</li><li>Info
3</li></ul>")
```

The ability to use HTML in a pop up comes in handy when you have a lot of details to add. It allows the use of images and links in pop ups. The following screenshot shows the HTML-formatted pop up added to a marker on the map:

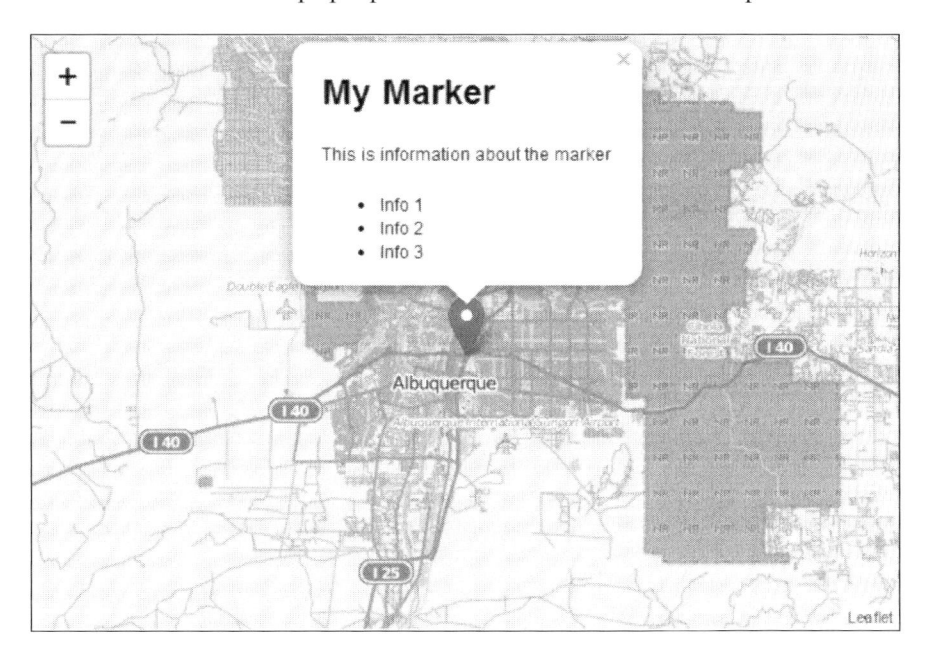

Creating Maps with Leaflet

You can also create an instance of the popup class and then assign it to multiple objects:

```
var mypopup = L.popup({keepInView:true,closeButton:false})
.setContent("<h1>My Marker</h1><p>This is information about the
marker</p><ul><li>Info 1</li><li>Info 2</li><li>Info 3</li></ul>");
marker.bindPopup(mypopup);
marker2.bindPopup(mypopup);
```

In the preceding code, you create an instance of the L.popup() class and assign it to the variable mypopup. Then, you can call the bindPopup() method on marker and marker2 with mypopup as the parameter. Both markers will have the same pop up content and options.

In the last section of this chapter, you will learn how to create a function that allows you to create a pop up with options and pass the content as a parameter.

Mobile mapping

The maps you have made so far have been tested on the desktop. One of the benefits of mapping in JavaScript is that mobile devices can run the code in a standard web browser without any external applications or plugins. Leaflet runs on mobile devices, such as iPhone, iPad, and Android devices. Any web page with a Leaflet map will work on a mobile device without any changes; however, you probably want to customize the map for mobile devices so that it works and looks like it was built specifically for mobile.

Lastly, the L.map() class has a locate() method, which uses the W3C Geolocation API. The Geolocation API allows you to find and track a user's location using the IP address, the wireless network information, or the GPS on a device. You do not need to know how to use the API; Leaflet handles all of this when you call locate().

HTML and CSS

The first step in converting your Leaflet map to a mobile version is to have it display properly on mobile devices. You can always tell when you open a website on your phone whether the developer took the time to make it mobile-accessible. How many times have you been on a website where the page loads and all you can see is the top-left corner, and you have to zoom around to read the page. It is not a good user experience. In LeafletEssentials.html in the <head> tag after the <link> tag for the CSS file, add the following code:

```
<style>

body{
padding: 0;
margin: 0;
    }
html, body, #map {
height: 100%;
        }
</style>
```

In the preceding CSS code, you set the `padding` and `margin` values to `0`. Think of a web page as a box model, where each element exists in its own box. Each box has a margin, which is the space between it and other boxes, and also padding, which is the space between the content inside the box and the box border (even if a border is not physically drawn). Setting the `padding` and `margin` values to `0` makes the `<body>` content fit to the size of the page. Lastly, you set the `height` value of the `<html>`, `<body>`, and `<div id = 'map'>` elements to `100%`.

> In CSS, # is the ID selector. In the code, #map is telling us to select the element with the `id = 'map'` line. In this case, it is our `<div>` element that holds the map.

The following diagram shows an overview of the settings for the web page:

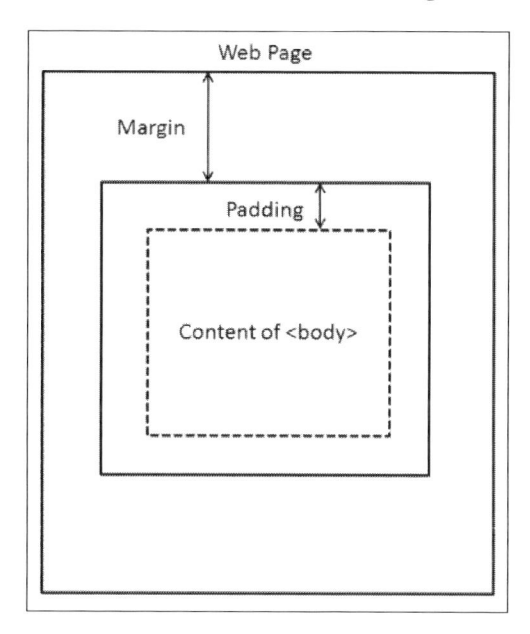

[Diagram showing a box model with "Web Page" as the outer box, "Margin" between the outer box and an inner box labeled "Padding", and a dashed inner box labeled "Content of <body>".]

The last step is to add the following code in the `<head>` section and after the `</title>` element:

```
<meta name="viewport" content="width=device-width, initial-scale=1.0, maximum-scale=1.0, user-scalable=no">
```

The preceding code modifies the viewport that the site is seen through. This code sets the viewport to the width of the device and renders it by a ratio of 1:1. Lastly, it disables the ability to resize the web page. This, however, does not affect your ability to zoom on the map.

Creating a mobile map with JavaScript

Now that you have configured the web page to render properly on mobile devices, it is time to add the JavaScript code that will grab the user's current location. For this, perform the following steps:

1. Create the map instance, but do not use `setView`:

   ```
   var map = L.map('map');
   ```

2. Add a tile layer:

   ```
   L.tileLayer('http://{s}.tile.osm.org/{z}/{x}/{y}.png').addTo(map);
   ```

3. Define a function to successfully find the location:

   ```
   Function foundLocation(e){}
   ```

4. Define a function to unsuccessfully find the location:

   ```
   functionnotFoundLocation(e){}
   ```

5. Add an event listener for `foundLocation()` and `notFoundLocation()`:

   ```
   map.on('locationfound', foundLocation);
   map.on('locationerror', notFoundLocation);
   ```

6. Use locate() to set the map view:

   ```
   map.locate({setView: true, maxZoom:10});
   ```

Chapter 1

The code creates the map and adds a tile layer. It then skips over the functions and event listeners and tries to locate the user. If it is able to locate the user, it runs the code in `foundLocation()` and sets the view to the latitude and longitude of the user. If it does not locate the user, it executes the code in `notFoundLocation()` and displays a zoomed-out world map.

To make this example more usable, add the following code to `notFoundLocation()`:

```
function notFoundLocation(e){
alert("Unable to find your location. You may need to enable Geolocation.");}
```

The `alert()` function creates a pop up in the browser with the message passed as a parameter. Anytime that the browser is unable to locate the user, they will see the following message. While some devices do not have location capabilities, at times, they need to be allowed in their security settings:

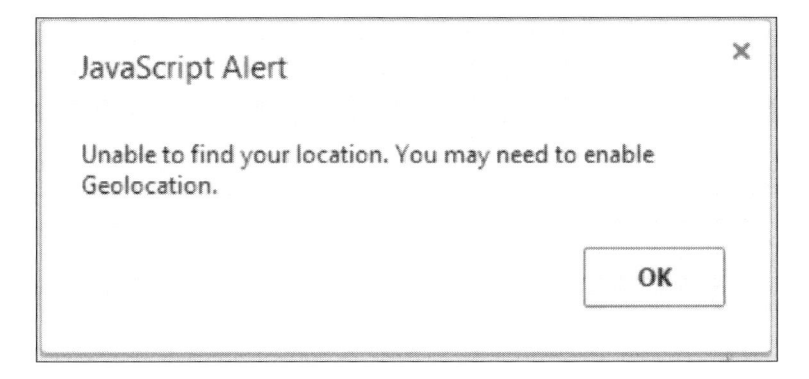

Now, add the following code to `foundLocation()`:

```
function foundLocation(e){
varmydate = new Date(e.timestamp);
L.marker(e.latlng).addTo(map).bindPopup(mydate.toString());
    }
```

Creating Maps with Leaflet

The preceding code will run when the user's location is found. The `e` in `foundLocation(e)` is an event object. It is sent when an event is triggered to the function that is responsible for handling that specific event type. It contains information about the event that you will want to know. In the preceding code, the first event object we grab is the `timestamp` object. If you were to display the timestamp in a pop up, you would get a bunch of numbers: **1400094289048**. The timestamp is the number of milliseconds that have passed since January 1, 1970 00:00:00 UTC. If you create an instance of the `date` class and pass it to the `timestamp` object, you receive a human-readable date. Next, the code creates a marker. The latitude and longitude are stored in `e.latlng`. You then add the marker to the map and bind a pop up. The pop up needs a string as a parameter, so you can use the `toString()` method of the `date` class or use `String(mydate)` to convert it. The following screenshot shows the pop up with the date and time when the user clicked on it:

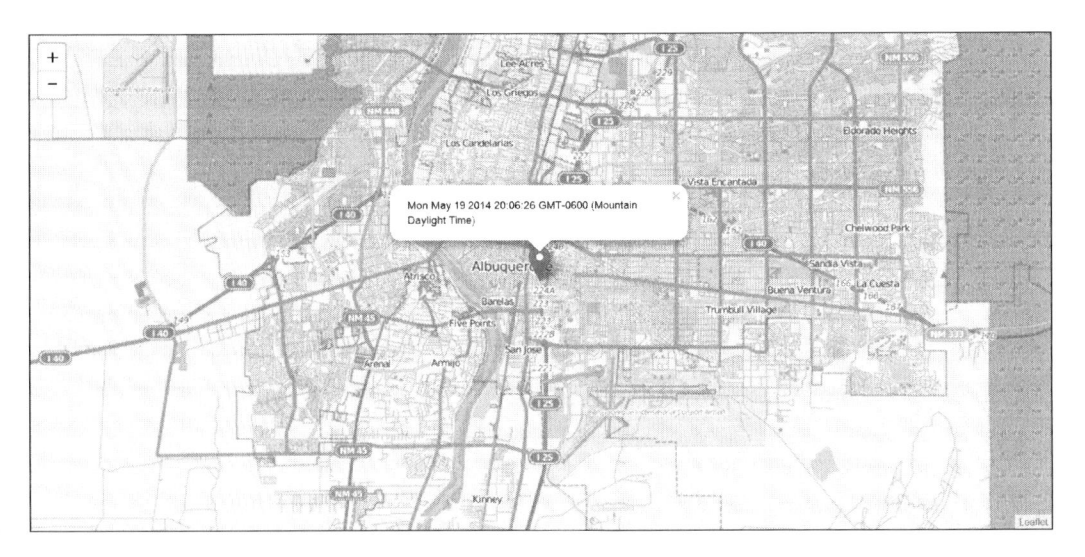

Events and event handlers

So far, you have created maps that display data and added a pop up that displayed when the user clicked on a marker. Now, you will learn how to handle other events and assign these events to event handler functions to process them and do something as a result.

[36]

You will first learn how to handle a `map` event. There are 34 events in the `map` class that can be subscribed to. This example will focus on the `click` event. To subscribe to an event, you use the event method `.on()`; so, for a `map` event, you use the `map.on()` method and pass the parameters as the event and function to handle the event. This is shown in the following code:

```
map.on('click', function(){alert("You clicked the map");});
```

The code tells Leaflet to send an alert pop-up box with the text **You clicked the map** when the user clicks on the map. In the mobile example, you created a listener that had a named function that executed `foundLocation()`. In the preceding code, the function was put in as a parameter. This is known as an anonymous function. The function has no name, and so, it can only be called when the user clicks on the map.

Remember `e` from the mobile example? If you pass `e` to the function, you can get the `longlat` value of the spot that the user clicked on, as shown in the following code:

```
map.on('click',function(e){
var coord=e.latlng.toString().split(',');
var lat=coord[0].split('(');
var long=coord[1].split(')');
alert("you clicked the map at LAT: "+ lat[1]+" and LONG:"+long[0])
});
```

The preceding code is spaced in a way that is more readable, but you can put it all on a single line. The code displays the longitude and latitude of the spot where the user clicked on the map. The second line assigns the variable `coord`, the value of `e.latlng`. The next two lines strip the latitude and longitude from the value so that you can display them clearly.

You can build on this example by adding a marker when the user clicks on the map by simply replacing the code with the following:

```
L.marker(e.latlng).addTo(map);
```

The preceding code is identical to the code in the mobile example. The difference is that in the mobile example, it was only executed when `locate()` was successful. In this example, it is executed every time the user clicks on the map.

In the section on markers, you created a marker that had the property `draggable:true`. Markers have three events that deal with dragging: `dragstart`, `drag`, and `dragend`. Perform the following steps to return the longitude and latitude of the marker in a pop up on `dragend`:

1. Create the marker and set the draggable property to `true`:

   ```
   varmyMarker = L.marker([35.10418, -
   106.62987],{title:"MyPoint",alt:"The Big
   I",draggable:true}).addTo(map);
   ```

2. Write a function to bind a pop up to the marker and call the method `getLatLong()`:

   ```
   myMarker.bindPopup("I have been moved to:
   "+String(myMarker.getLatLng()));
   ```

3. Subscribe to the event:

   ```
   myMarker.on('dragend',whereAmI);
   ```

Open the map and click on the marker. Hold down the left mouse button and drag the marker to a new location on the map. Release the left button and click on the marker again to trigger the pop up. The pop up will have the new latitude and longitude of the marker.

Custom functions

You subscribed to an event and handled it with a function. So far, you have only passed e as a parameter. In JavaScript, you can send anything you want to the function. Also, functions can be called anywhere in your code. You do not have to call them only in response to an event. In this short example, you will create a function that returns a pop up and is triggered on a call and not by an event.

First, create a marker and bind a pop up to it. For the content of the pop up, enter `createPopup(Text as a parameter)`. Add the marker to the map as shown in the following code:

```
var marker1 = L.marker([35.10418, -
106.62987]).addTo(map).bindPopup(createPopup("Text as a
parameter"));
```

Create a second marker and set the content of the pop up to `createPopup (Different text as a parameter)`:

```
var marker2 = L.marker([35, -
106]).addTo(map).bindPopup(createPopup("Different text as a
parameter"));
```

In the previous examples, you created a pop up by passing text or a pop-up instance. In this example, you call a function, `createPopup()`, with a string as a parameter, as shown in the following code:

```
functioncreatePopup(x){
return
L.popup({keepInView:true,closeButton:false}).setContent(x);functio
n createPopup(x){
returnL.popup({keepInView:true,closeButton:false}).setContent(x);
}
```

The function takes a parameter called x. In the marker, when you call the function, you pass a string. This is sent to the function and stored as x. When the pop up is created, the `setContent()` method is given the value of x instead of a hardcoded string. This function is useful if you have a lot of options set on your pop ups and want them all to be the same. It limits the number of times that you need to repeat the same code. Just pass the text of the pop up to the function, and you get a new pop up with the standardized formatting options. The following screenshot shows both of the pop ups generated by the custom function:

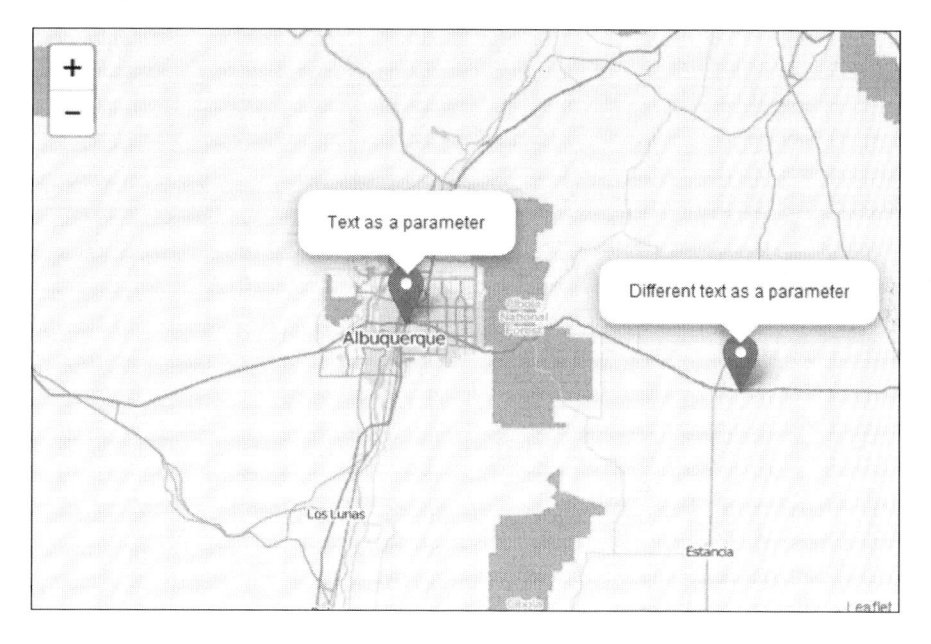

Summary

This chapter covered almost every major topic required to create a Leaflet map. You learned how to add tile layers from multiple providers, including satellite imagery. You can now add points, lines, and polygons to the map, as well as collections of polylines and polygons. You can group layers of different types into layer or feature collections. This chapter covered the styling of objects and adding pop ups. You learned how to interact with the user by responding to events and created custom functions to allow you to code more by writing less.

In the next chapter, you will learn how to add GeoJSON data to your map.

2
Mapping GeoJSON Data

In *Chapter 1*, *Creating Maps with Leaflet*, all of the geometry elements—points, lines, and polygons—were created one at a time. You learned how to create groups of features using layer and feature groups and also multipolyline and multipolygon classes. In this chapter, you will learn how to add GeoJSON data to your map. The data will be comprised of multiple geometries and will have descriptive data associated with it.

In this chapter, we will cover the following topics:

- What is GeoJSON?
- How to add it to your map
- How to style it
- Iterating through features
- How to call GeoJSON from external sources

Understanding the roots of GeoJSON

Before GeoJSON, there was **JavaScript Object Notation (JSON)**, and before JSON, there was **Extensible Markup Language (XML)**. As computers started to talk to each other over the Internet, the ability to send data from a service to a client became more important. XML, JSON, and GeoJSON are formats that represent and transmit data. XML was an attempt at a human-readable format that could store and send data. XML uses opening and closing tags to separate data. JSON is an alternative to XML that more closely resembles the way objects are created in JavaScript. JSON uses key-value pairs and is usually smaller than XML.

Exploring GeoJSON

GeoJSON is a JSON format that encodes geometries. GeoJSON can encode points, line strings, and polygons. It also allows for multipart geometries. You can encode multipoints, multiline strings, and multipolygons. These should sound familiar because they are pretty close to the geometries you learned to draw in *Chapter 1*, *Creating Maps with Leaflet*. The following GeoJSON code shows you two points in a feature collection:

```
{"type":"FeatureCollection",
  "features":[
    {"type":"Feature",
      "geometry":{
        "type":"Point",
        "coordinates":[-106.62987,35.10418]
        },
      "properties":{
        "name":"My Point",
        "title":"A point at the Big I"
        }
    },   {"type":"Feature",
      "geometry":{
        "type":"Point",
        "coordinates":[-106,35]
        },
      "properties":{
        "name":"MyOther Point",
        "title":"A point near Moriarty and I40"
        }
    }
  ]
}
```

The feature collection in the preceding code is not a geometry, but rather a collection of geometries similar to the feature layer described in *Chapter 1*, *Creating Maps with Leaflet*.

To view the full GeoJSON specification, you can go to `http://geojson.org/geojson-spec.html`.

> For tools that can help you write and check your JSON, see `http://www.jsoneditoronline.org/` or `http://geojsonlint.com/`.

GeoJSON in Leaflet.js

GeoJSON is just another data format for you to add to your map. It can be added as a hardcoded variable. Leaflet.js geometries—markers, polylines, and polygons—can be converted to GeoJSON. You can style the data, apply options to each feature, and even filter the data. The next sections will cover these topics, starting with adding GeoJSON as a hardcoded variable.

GeoJSON as a variable

The easiest way to add GeoJSON to your map is to hardcode the data into a variable. In Leaflet.js, you will start by creating a variable that will contain GeoJSON. In the following code, GeoJSON data consisting of two points is assigned to the `geojson` variable:

```
vargeojson = [{
"type": "Feature",
"geometry": {
"type": "Point",
"coordinates": [-106.62987,35.10418]
        },
   "properties": {
    "name": "My Point",
    "title": "A point at the Big I"
        }
},{
"type": "Feature",
  "geometry": {
      "type": "Point",
       "coordinates": [-106, 35]
               },
"properties": {
      "name": "My Other Point",
       "title": "A point near Moriarty and I40"
               }
}];
```

Once you have the GeoJSON data in a variable, as shown in the preceding code, adding it to the map is no different from adding any other geometry you have learned so far. The following code adds GeoJSON to the map:

```
vargeoJsonLayer = L.geoJson(geojson).addTo(map);
```

Mapping GeoJSON Data

The preceding code creates a `geoJsonLayer` variable. This variable is an instance of the `L.geoJson()` class. It takes a variable with the GeoJSON data as a parameter and then you chain `.addTo(map)` to the end.

> Objects have been created using (`latitude, longitude`) in *Chapter 1, Creating Maps with Leaflet*; however, note that in GeoJSON, the format is (`longitude, latitude`).

The result of this code will be a map with two markers, as shown in the following screenshot:

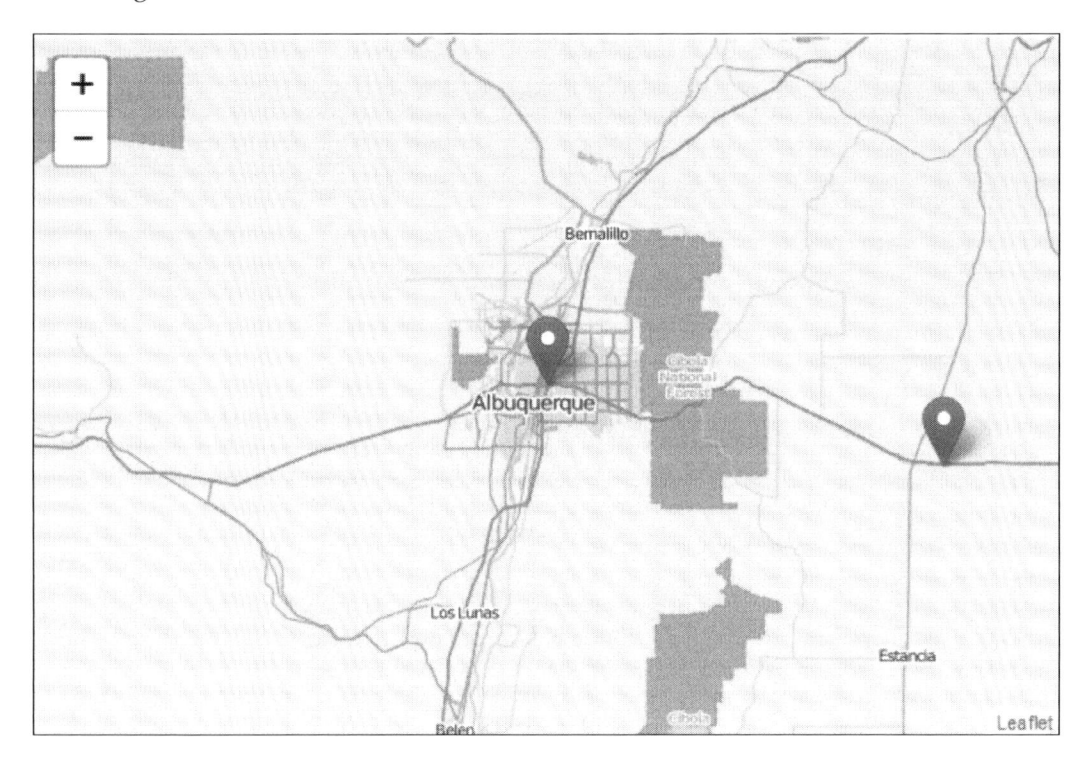

Multiple geometries in GeoJSON

In the preceding example, GeoJSON contained only points. While it is common for a GeoJSON file to contain a single geographic feature, it is not a requirement. Leaflet.js can load GeoJSON with multiple geometries in a single GeoJSON file. In this example, you will learn how to create and add a GeoJSON file with a point, line string, and polygon. The following GeoJSON code contains three different geometries:

```
vargeojson = [{
"type": "Feature",
"geometry": {
"type": "Point",
"coordinates": [-106.62987, 35.10418]
        },
  "properties": {
  "name": "My Point",
        "title": "A point at the Big I"
        }
},{
"type": "Feature",
  "geometry": {
      "type": "LineString",
        "coordinates":[[-106.67999, 35.14097],
                      [-106.68892, 35.12974],
  [-106.69064, 35.1098]]
             },
"properties": {
     "name": "My LineString",
     "title": "A line along the Rio Grande"
             }
},{
"type": "Feature",
  "geometry": {
      "type": "Polygon",
       "coordinates":[[[-106.78059, 35.14574],
           [-106.7799, 35.10559],
           [-106.71467, 35.13704],
           [-106.69716, 35.17942],
           [-106.78059, 35.14574]]]
             },
"properties": {
     "name": "My Polygon",
     "title": "Balloon Fiesta Park"
             }
  }];
```

Mapping GeoJSON Data

To create different geometries in a single GeoJSON file, you just need to specify the type and include the proper coordinates, as shown in the preceding code. For a line string, you must include at least two points. In Leaflet.js, polygons do not require you to close them by including the starting coordinates at the end of the list. GeoJSON does require you to close the polygon. The polygon in the preceding code starts and ends with `[-106.78059, 35.14574]`. The preceding code will produce the map shown in the following screenshot:

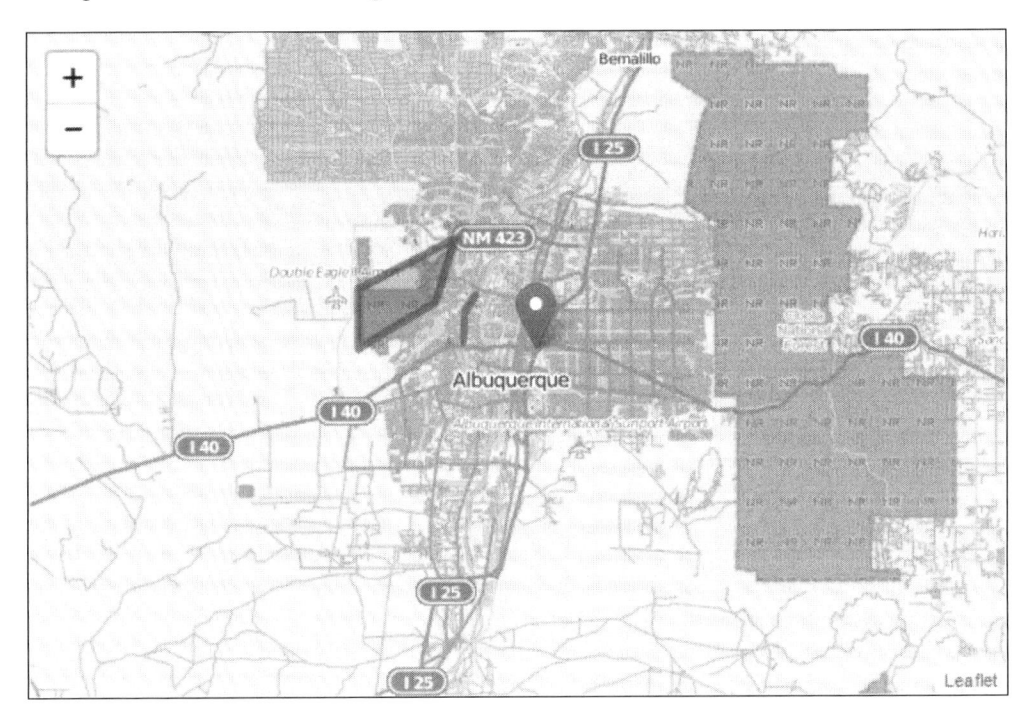

Polygons with holes

A polygon in GeoJSON can be a donut, that is, you can cut a polygon out of the middle of another polygon. The following code shows you a polygon feature with two polygons, the outer and inner polygons:

```
vargeojson = [{
"type": "Feature",
  "geometry": {
     "type": "Polygon",
      "coordinates":[
         [[-106.875, 35.20074],
         [-106.82281, 34.9895],
         [-106.50146, 35.00525],
```

```
            [-106.47949, 35.1985],
            [-106.875, 35.20074]],
    [[-106.6745, 35.1463],
    [-106.70403, 35.05192],
    [-106.55296, 35.05979],
    [-106.53854, 35.17212],
    [-106.6745, 35.1463]]
        ]
                    },
    "properties": {
        "name": "My Polygon with a hole",
        "title": "Donut"
                    }
        }];
```

In the preceding code, the first set of points creates a four-sided polygon. The second set of points—the next level of indentation—creates a four-sided polygon in the middle of the first polygon. The result is shown in the following screenshot:

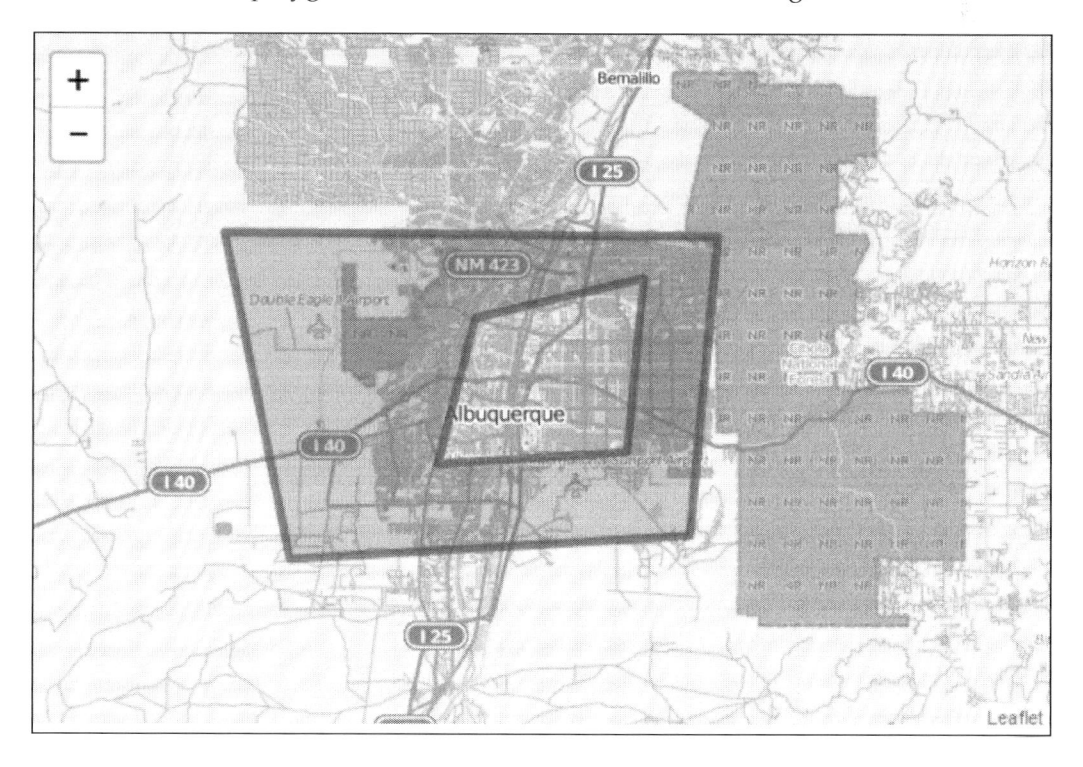

The middle of the polygon in the preceding screenshot is hollow. If you add a pop up to the polygon, it will only open when you click on the blue ring.

Mapping GeoJSON Data

GeoJSON from Leaflet.js objects

Each of the geometries you learned about in *Chapter 1, Creating Maps with Leaflet*, have a `toGeoJson()` method. This method will convert the geometry to a GeoJSON object that can be added to the map. The following code shows you how to convert a marker to a GeoJSON layer:

```
varmyMarker=L.marker([35.10418, -106.62987]);
varmarkerAsGeoJSON = myMarker.toGeoJSON();
vargeoJsonLayer = L.geoJson(markerAsGeoJSON).addTo(map);
```

The preceding code creates a marker, as you did in the *Adding data to your map* section in *Chapter 1, Creating Maps with Leaflet*. Secondly, it calls the `.toGeoJSON()` method, which returns a GeoJSON object and stores it as `markerAsGeoJSON`. Lastly, `markerAsGeoJSON` is added to the map as GeoJSON.

Styling GeoJSON layers

GeoJSON layers have a `style` option and a `setStyle()` method. Using the `style` option, you specify a function that will style the layer. The following code shows you how to style a GeoJSON layer with the `style` option:

```
functionstyleFunction(feature){
switch (feature.properties.type) {
case 'LineString': return {color: "red"}; break;
case 'Polygon':    return {color: "purple"}; break;
        }
}
vargeoJsonLayer =
L.geoJson(geojson,{style:styleFunction}).addTo(map);
```

The preceding code creates a style function that returns a color based on the GeoJSON feature names. If it is a line string, it is colored red, and if it is a polygon, it is colored purple.

> You can also style the GeoJSON data using other options such as `stroke`, `weight`, `opacity`, and `fillColor`. The full list is available at http://leafletjs.com/reference.html#path-options.

Chapter 2

The last line creates the GeoJSON layer, calls the style function, and then adds it to the map. The result is seen in the following screenshot:

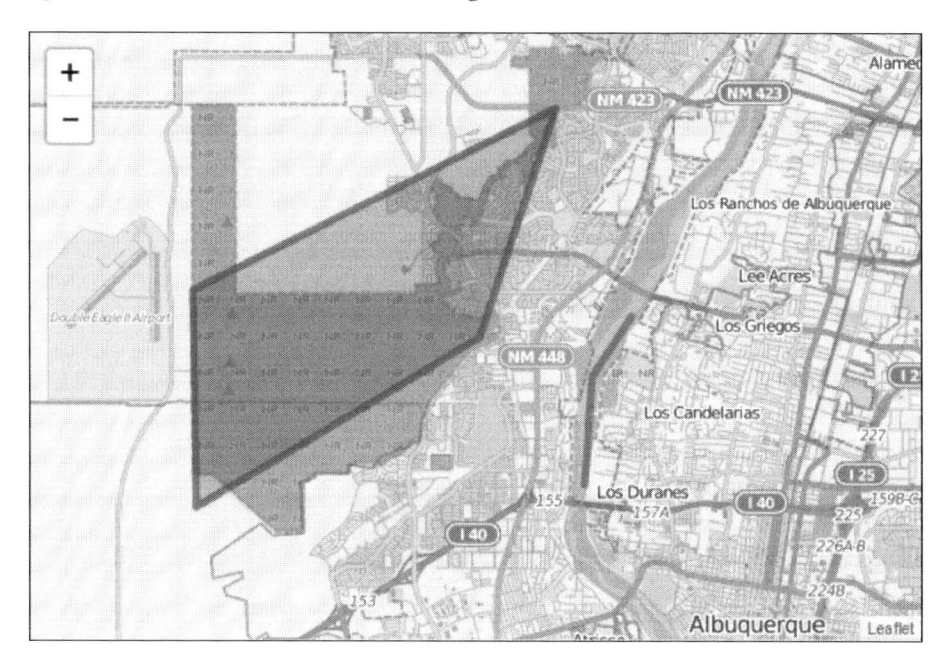

The `setStyle()` method allows you to change the style after one has already been applied or by using events. The following code shows you how an event can call the `setStyle()` method to update the color of the GeoJSON layer:

```
functionstyleFunction(){return {color: "purple"}; }
functionnewStyle(){geoJsonLayer.setStyle({color:"green"});}

vargeoJsonLayer =
L.geoJson(geojson,{style:styleFunction}).addTo(map);
geoJsonLayer.on('mouseover',newStyle);
geoJsonLayer.on('mouseout',function(e){geoJsonLayer.resetStyle(e.t
arget);});
```

The preceding code first creates a function called `styleFunction()`, which is called in the fourth line of code using the `style` option as shown in the previous example. It sets the color of the GeoJSON layer to `purple`. Next, there is another function, `newStyle()`, which sets the color to `green`. Lastly, there are two events: `mouseover` and `mouseout`. When the user hovers over the GeoJSON layer, the `newStyle()` function is called and the layer is colored green. As soon as the mouse moves off the layer, an anonymous function is called. This function uses the GeoJSON method, `resetStyle()`, to pass the target of the event—the GeoJSON layer—and changes the layer back to its original style.

Consider the following example code:

```
function styleFunction(){return {color: "purple"}; }
function newStyle(){geoJsonLayer.setStyle({color:"green"});}
function oldStyle(){geoJsonLayer.setStyle({color:"purple"});}
var geoJsonLayer =
L.geoJson(geojson,{style:styleFunction}).addTo(map);
geoJsonLayer.on('mouseover',newStyle);geoJsonLayer.
on('mouseout',oldStyle);
```

The preceding code first creates a function called `styleFunction()`, which is called in the fourth line of code using the `style` option as shown in the previous example. It sets the color of the GeoJSON layer to `purple`. Next, there are two other functions: `newStyle()` and `oldStyle()`. The former sets the color to `green` and the latter returns the color back to the original `purple`. Lastly, there are two events that call the style functions: `mouseover` and `mouseout`. When the user hovers over the GeoJSON layer, the `newStyle()` function is called and the layer is colored `green`. As soon as the mouse moves off the layer, `oldStyle()` is called and the color is set back to `purple`.

Iterating through the features

In Leaflet.js, you can iterate through the features in a GeoJSON file and perform actions on it before it is added to the map. This can be done with the `onEachFeature`, `pointToLayer`, or `filter` option.

Attaching pop ups with onEachFeature

The GeoJSON layer in Leaflet.js has an `onEachFeature` option, which is called for every feature in the data. This can be used to bind a pop up to each feature as it is added to the map. The following code uses the onEachFeature option to bind a pop up:

```
L.geoJson(geojson, {
onEachFeature: function(feature,layer) {
layer.bindPopup(feature.properties.title);
     }
}).addTo(map);
```

Chapter 2

In the preceding code, an anonymous function is called on each feature. The function binds a pop up in line three with the value of the feature's `title` property. You can select any one of a feature's properties using `feature.properties.NameOfProperty`. The result is shown in the following screenshot:

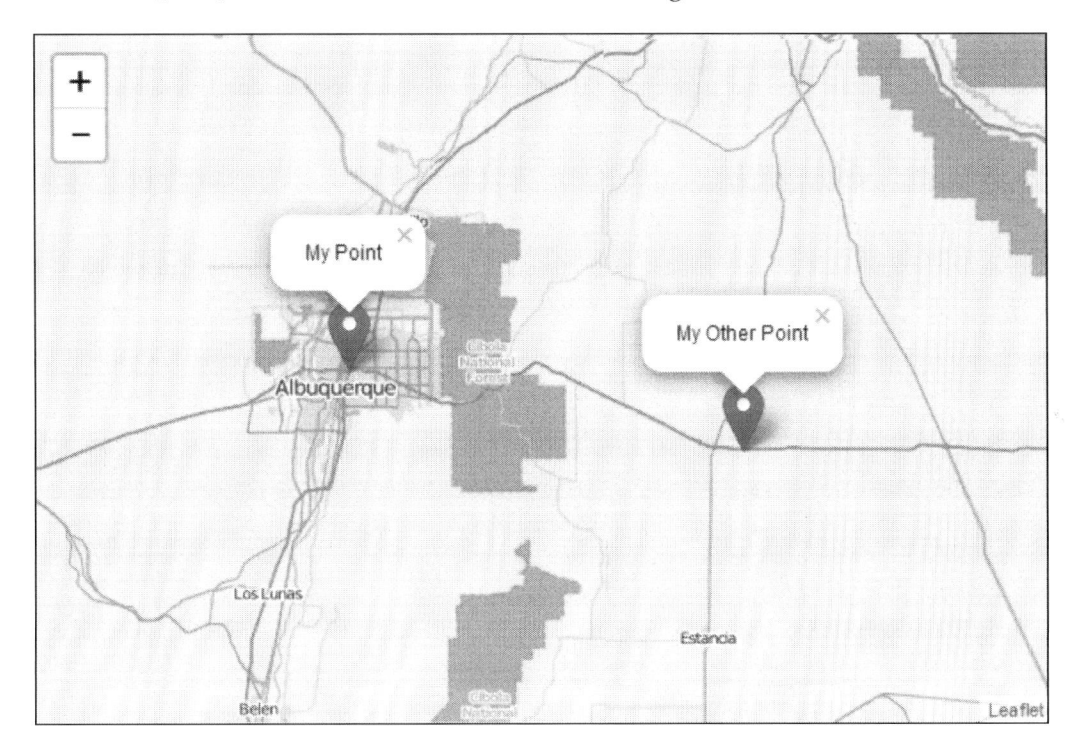

Creating layers from points with pointToLayer

The `pointToLayer` option works with points, as they are handled differently as compared to polylines and polygons. In the following code, a marker is created and styled for each feature based on the name of the feature:

```
var options2 = {
draggable: false,
title: "A point near Moriarty and I40"
};
var x;
var y;
L.geoJson(geojsonFeature, {
pointToLayer: function(feature,latlng) {
switch (feature.properties.name) {
case "My Point": x = L.marker(latlng,{draggable:true,title:"A point at the
```

[51]

Mapping GeoJSON Data

```
    Big I"}).bindPopup(feature.properties.name); return x;
case "My Other Point":   y =
L.marker(latlng,options2).bindPopup(feature.properties.name);
return y;
        }
     }
}).addTo(map);
```

The preceding code starts by creating a JSON variable that holds the style information. Next, the layers on which the markers will be created are created as x and y. Then, the GeoJSON layer is created and the `pointToLayer` option is called with an anonymous function. The function has a `switch` statement that styles the markers based on their `name` property. The first `case` statement has the property information added at the creation of the marker. The second `case` statement passes the JSON variable with the style information. Both work, so if you have a style that you want to apply to all your features, you can write it once in a variable and call it during the creation of the marker. Because the code assigned the layers to variables x and y, you can add or remove layers using `map.removeLayer(x)`.

Displaying a subset of data with filter

There might be times when you load in GeoJSON from an outside source and you do not want to display all the features in the data. Filtering will allow you to not display certain features based on criteria that you set. Modifying the `case` statement in the previous point-to-layer example, you will learn how to filter data based on the name of the feature. The following code shows you how to do this:

```
L.geoJson(geojsonFeature, {
filter: function(feature,latlng) {
switch (feature.properties.name) {
case "My Point": return true;
case "My Other Point":   return false;
        }
     }
}).addTo(map);
```

The preceding code should look similar to the previous examples. You create the GeoJSON layer and then pass the `filter` option. The option uses an anonymous function. The function, in this case, is a `switch` statement that takes the name of the feature as a parameter. Since the function is deciding on whether or not to display a feature, the return value is a Boolean. In this example, if the name of the feature is `My Other Point`, it will not be displayed. The following screenshot shows you the result; only one marker is added to the map:

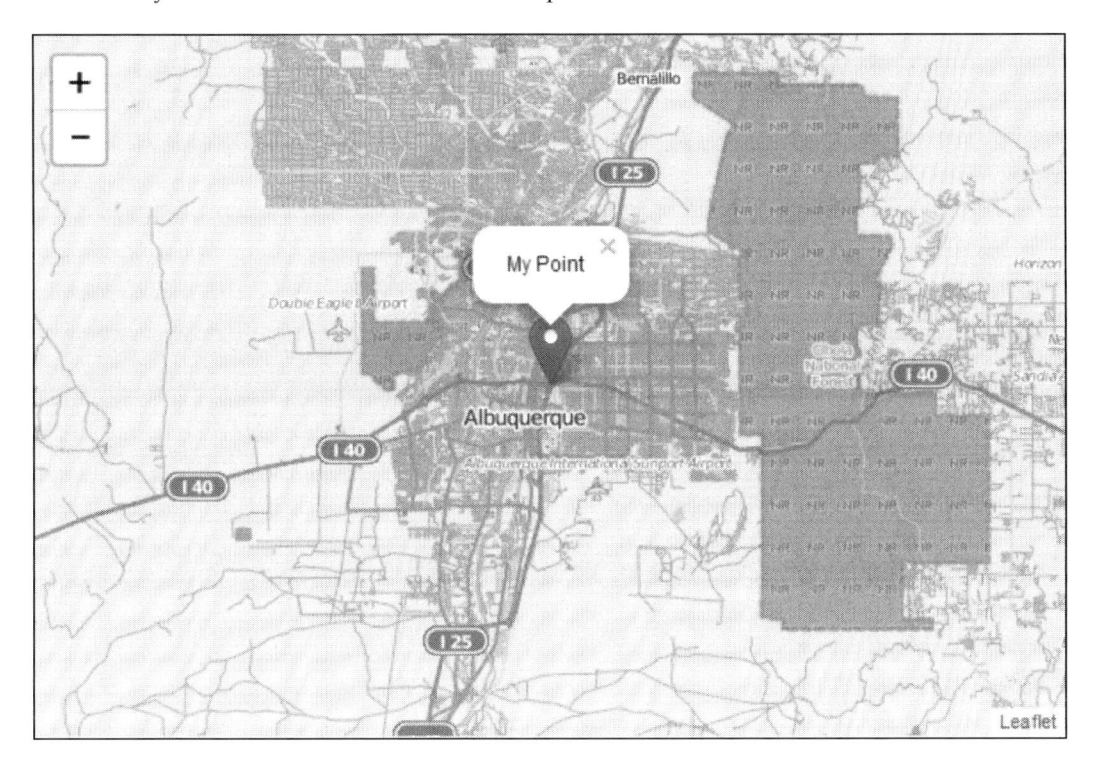

Summary

In this chapter, you learned how to add and style a GeoJSON layer in Leaflet.js. Finally, you learned how to iterate through the features in a GeoJSON file and perform an action such as binding a pop up or applying a style based on a property in the feature. GeoJSON is a popular and common data format. Knowing how to use it in Leaflet.js is an important skill. This chapter gave you a solid foundation with which you can continue to learn about GeoJSON.

In the next chapter, you will learn how to create heatmaps using several available plugins.

3
Creating Heatmaps and Choropleth Maps

In the first two chapters, you learned how to make a map and add points, lines, polygons, and even GeoJSON. Now, you will use these skills to create two types of thematic maps: heatmaps and choropleth maps. These maps show you concentrations of points or statistical variables using two different styles of representations.

In this chapter, we will cover the following topics:

- What is a heatmap?
- How do I create a heatmap?
- What is a choropleth map?
- How do I create a choropleth map?

What is a heatmap?

A heatmap is a color-coded grid added to a map. The colors usually range from cool colors, such as blue, to hot colors, such as yellow, orange, and red. Heatmaps represent point data in one of two ways: density or intensity. In a density map, the grid is colored red when multiple points are in close proximity of each other and blue when dispersed. High concentrations of points create the heat. In an intensity map, points are assigned a value or an intensity score. The higher the score or intensity, the hotter the color in the grid at the location of the point; inversely, the lower the score, the cooler the grid color at the point location.

> Heatmaps are created by placing a grid over the map and calculating the points within an area through a process called Multivariate Kernel Density Estimation. For a detailed explanation and the exact formulas used, you can visit http://en.wikipedia.org/wiki/Multivariate_kernel_density_estimation.

Heatmaps with Leaflet.heat

The first heatmap you will make will be a density heatmap, using the `Leaflet.heat` plugin. You can download the JavaScript plugin at https://github.com/Leaflet/Leaflet.heat. The following steps will walk you through creating your first heatmap:

1. Using `LeafletEssentials.html`, add a reference to `Leaflet.heat.js` with either a URL to a remote copy or the path to your local copy, as shown in the following code:

   ```
   <script src="http://Leaflet.github.io/Leaflet.heat/dist/Leaflet-heat.js"></script> or,
   <script src="Leaflet-heat.js"></script>
   ```

2. Add an array of points. Your points can contain additional information but must have the latitude and longitude as the first two elements. The following code shows you three points from the code. The full code contains many more, which will allow you to create the heatmap:

   ```
   var points = [
   [35.1555 , -106.591838 , "<img src='http://farm8.staticflickr.com/7153/6831137393_fa38634fd7_m.jpg'>"],
   [35.0931 , -106.664177 , "<img src='http://farm3.staticflickr.com/2167/2479129916_0d861b2600.jpg'>"],
   [35.1143 , -106.577991 , "<img src='http://farm2.staticflickr.com/1416/908720823_e390a242f4.jpg'>"]];
   ```

3. Lastly, create the heat layer and add it to the map:

   ```
   var heat = L.heatLayer(points).addTo(map);
   ```

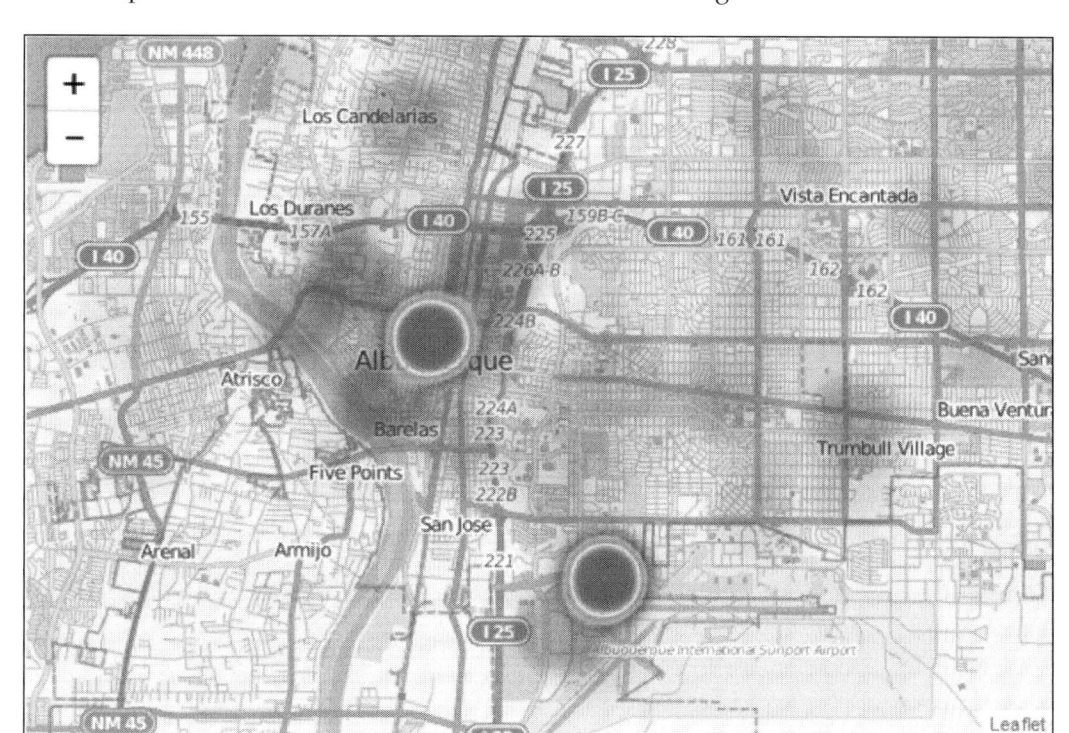

Your map should look like what is shown in the following screenshot:

The preceding screenshot is the default heatmap; it's not very stylish.

Using options to style your map

`Leaflet.heat` allows you to pass options to the constructor. The options are as follows:

- `MaxZoom`
- `Max`
- `Radius`
- `Blur`
- `Gradient`

The most important options are `blur`, `maxZoom`, and `radius`.

Changing the blur value

Blur merges the points the together, or not. A low blur value will create individual points, whereas a higher number will make the points merge with each other and look more fluid. Blur too much and you will wash out your points. The following screenshots show you different blur values.

The following screenshot shows you the blur value set to 1:

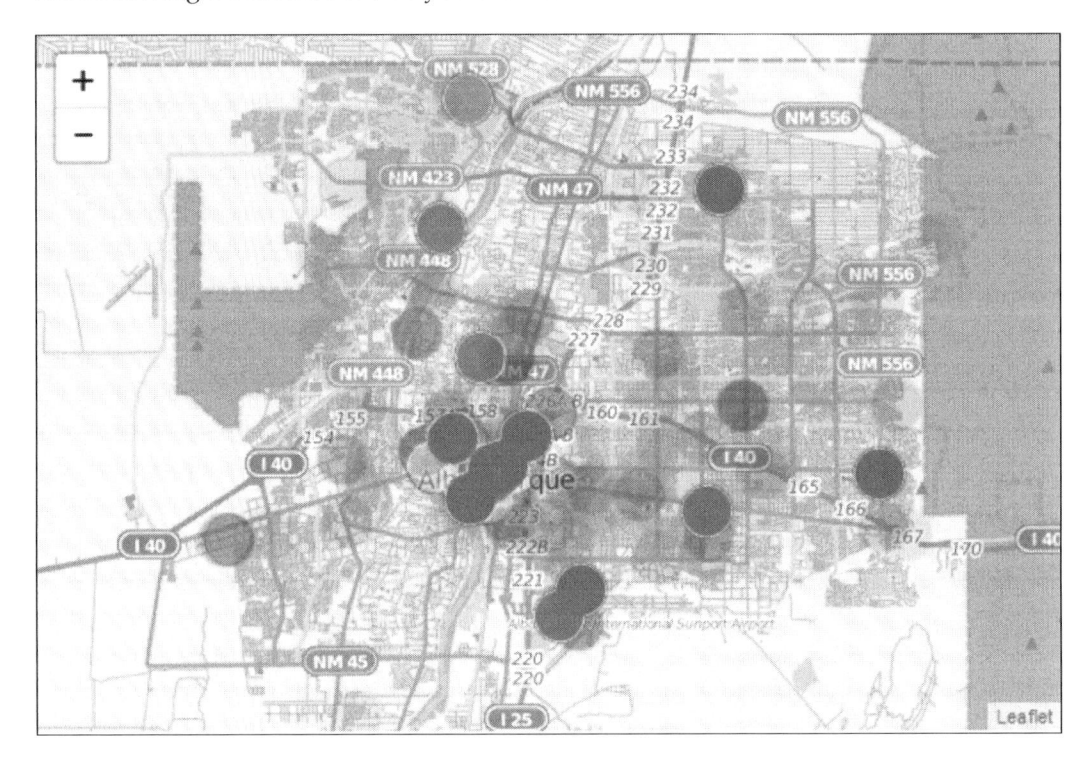

The following screenshot shows you the blur value set to 40:

The following screenshot shows you the blur value set to `80`:

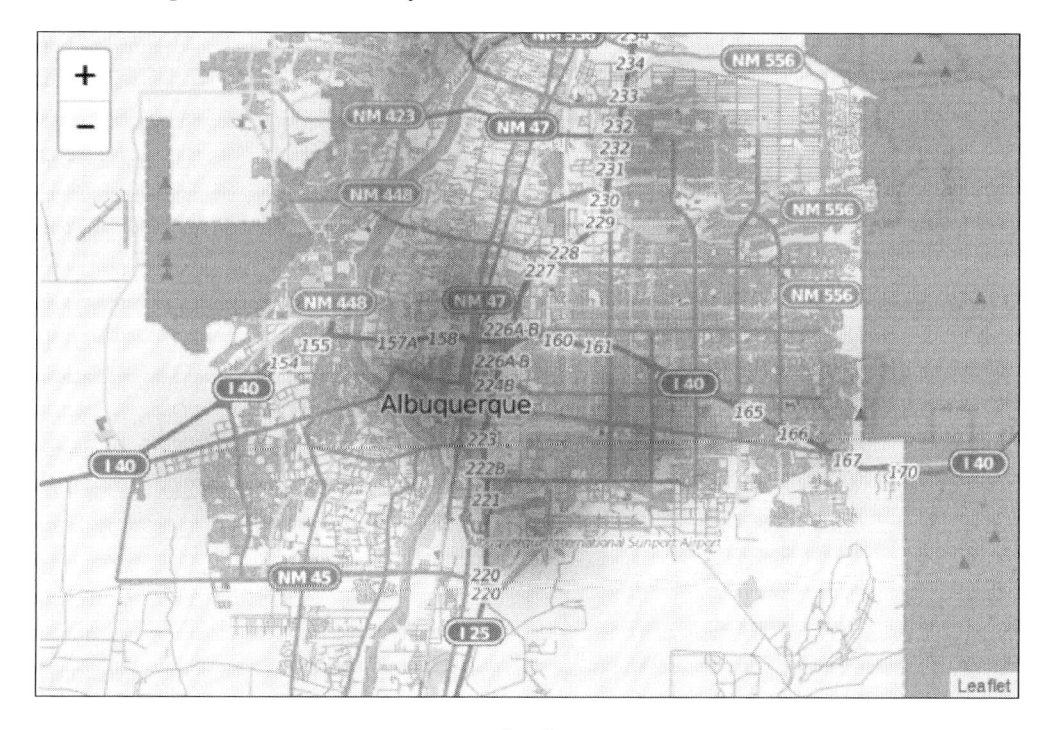

[59]

Notice how at `80`, the blur takes away any hotspots on the map; it is washed out. It will take some to adjust to finding the perfect value. Starting with the default value of `15` is a good idea.

Changing the maxZoom value

The `maxZoom` option sets the points to their maximum intensity at the specified zoom. If you set the `maxZoom` option of the map, you can ignore this setting. You should set this to the zoom level where the map looks best. If you set it to too far out, the points will lose their heat as you zoom in, and if you make it too tight of a zoom, the user might not be able to see all the points on the map at once.

Changing the radius value

This option should be obvious. It adjusts the radius of the points. A small number makes a small point and a large number makes a large point. The amount of data points can affect the proper radius of your points. The more points you have, the smaller you could make each point and still have a readable map. Making the radius too large will create a large blob of values that will be hard to interpret.

Setting the gradient option

The `gradient` option allows you to specify the color at different levels. The default is set to `{.4:"blue",.6:"cyan",.7:"lime",.8:"yellow",1:"red"}`. You can specify ranges from `0` to `1`. The outermost color is `0` and the center is `1`. The default setting tends to be a common color range for heatmaps that most people understand. Leaving the default is the best option, but if you need to change the colors for some reason, you can.

> To create a color combination that is visually pleasing, you can use a tool such as Color Brewer 2. This is available at http://colorbrewer2.org/.

Methods of Leaflet.heat

Along with the options to style your heatmap, `Leaflet.heat` has four methods as follows:

- `setOptions(options)`
- `addLatLng(latlng)`
- `setLatLngs(latlngs)`
- `redraw()`

[60]

You can reset the style, add new data, load in all new data, and redraw the map. The method you will use most is the `addLatLng()` method. This method allows you to append data to your map. In the previous example, you can add the following code as the last line:

```
heat.addLatLng([35,-106]);
```

The preceding code uses the `addLatLng()` method to add the point (35,-106) to the map. There is an excellent example of using an event with `addLatLng()` at http://Leaflet.github.io/Leaflet.heat/demo/draw.html. As you move the mouse, points are added to the map in real time.

> The `redraw()` method is called by `setOptions()`, `addLatLng()`, and `setLatLngs()` so that you do not need to call it after executing any of these methods.

If you want to show multiple datasets on a single map, you can write a custom function to add another set. The following code adds a dataset. You will need to populate the `newPoints` variable with your other dataset:

```
function add(){
heat.setLatLngs(newPoints);
}
heat.setLatLngs(newPoints);
```

In the preceding code, a dataset named `newPoints` is added to the map and the old dataset points are removed. In your HTML, create a button to execute the function:

```
<button onclick="addNewPoints()">Addonclick="add ()">Add New Points</button>
```

The preceding code is the HTML that calls the `addNewPoints()` function when it is clicked on.

Adding markers to the heatmap

You need a series of points to create the heatmap, so why not use them to attach a pop up to the heat layer. In the data, there was a latitude, longitude, and a third field that contained a URL to an image. The following code shows you how to turn that data into a marker with a pop up:

```
for(var i=0;i<points.length;i++)
{
L.marker([parseFloat(points[i][0]),parseFloat(points[i][1])],{opacity:0}).bindPopup(points[i][2],{keepInView:true}).addTo(map);
}
```

Creating Heatmaps and Choropleth Maps

The preceding code is a standard for a loop that starts with 0 and executes until you have iterated through all the points—`points.length`. This creates a marker by passing each point's latitude and longitude, `points[i][0]` and `points[i][1]`, and converts them to a float value. Next, the `opacity` option is set to 0. This makes the points invisible. The points are on the map, and they can be clicked on, but you cannot see them. This gives the appearance of the hotspot layer that contains the pop up. Lastly, the `bindPopup()` method is passed the URL to the image, `bindPopup(points[i][2])`, and is added to the map. The following screenshot shows you the pop up with the invisible markers and heat layer:

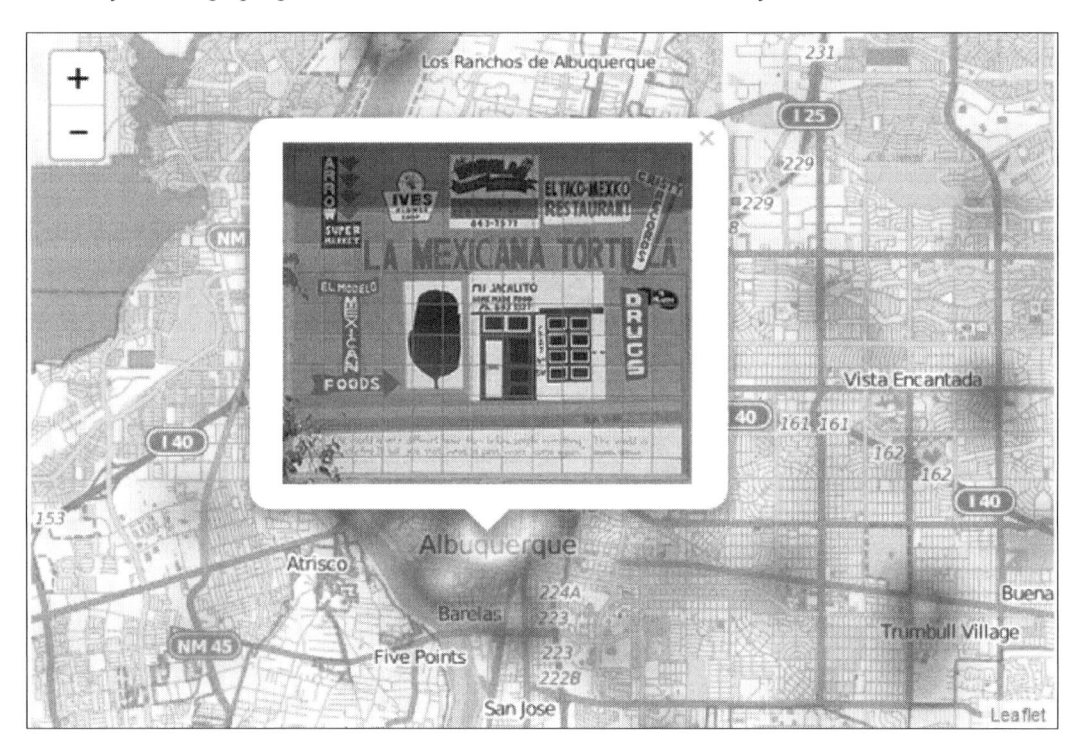

Creating heatmaps with heatmap.js

Creating a heatmap that uses intensity can be accomplished in Leaflet using `heatmap.js`. You can get `heatmap.js` at http://www.patrick-wied.at/static/heatmapjs/index.html. This includes the plugins for `leaflet.js` and other mapping packages. The process to create the heatmap is similar to the previous example. The following steps will walk you through creating a heatmap:

Chapter 3

1. Using `LeafletEssentials.html`, add a reference to `heatmap.js` and `heatmap-Leaflet` with either a URL to a remote copy or the path to your local copy, as shown in the following code:

   ```
   <script type="text/javascript" src="http://www.patrick-
   wied.at/static/heatmapjs/src/heatmap.js"></script>
   <script type="text/javascript" src="http://www.patrick-
   wied.at/static/heatmapjs/src/heatmap-Leaflet"></script>
   ```

2. Add a JavaScript object with the `max` value of the intensity and an array of data:

   ```
   Var myData={max: 46,
   data: [{lat: 33.5363, lon:-117.044, value: 1},{lat:
   33.5608, lon:-117.24, value: 1}]};
   ```

3. Create the heat layer and set the options:

   ```
   Var heatmapLayer = L.TileLayer.heatMap({
   radius: 20,
   opacity: 0.8,
   gradient: {
                   0.45: "rgb(0,0,255)",
                   0.55: "rgb(0,255,255)",
                   0.65: "rgb(0,255,0)",
                   0.95: "rgb(255,255,0)",
                   1.0: "rgb(255,0,0)"
               }
   });
   ```

4. Add the data to the map. Because the data is in an object, you use dot notation, referencing it as `objectname.data`; in this case, `myData.data`. You could also use `myData['data']`:

   ```
   heatmapLayer.addData(myData.data);
   ```

5. Lastly, modify your `map` object to add the layers:

   ```
   var map = new L.Map('map', {
   center: new L.LatLng(35,-106),
   zoom: 12,
   laycrs: [baseLayer, heatmapLayer]
               });
   ```

   > Please note that currently, you might need to reference an older version of Leaflet. This will be updated in a future version of the plugin.

[63]

Creating Heatmaps and Choropleth Maps

Your map should look like what is shown in the following screenshot:

Modifying the heatmap options

The heatmap allows you to modify three settings: radius, opacity, and gradient. Like the previous example, gradient controls the size of each point in the map. The opacity option allows you to specify a value between 0 and 1. 0 is completely transparent and the heatmap layer will not show up on the map. The value 1 will make the heatmap layer solid, and you will not be able to see what is underneath each point. Somewhere between .70 and .80 seems to be the perfect opacity to view the heat layer and the base layer underneath. Lastly, the gradient, while best left alone, can be modified by setting a value of 0 to 1 and assigning a color. Colors in the gradient can be RGB values, or you can use color names: red, yellow, blue, or lime.

Adding more data to the map

You will eventually need to add more data to the map after it has been drawn. To do this requires you to append values to the object and then add the object again. First, to add data to the JavaScript object, you can use the following code:

```
myData. push({lat:35,lon:-106,value:46});
```

[64]

The `myData` object has a key data that is an array. You reference it by using `myData.data[index]`. You might not know how many items are in the array, so using the length of the array as the index, you will always get the next available index. This works because the length is the number of items, but the index starts at 0. So, for a three-item array, the length is three but the last index is two. Using the length gives you the next empty index. Then, just assign a value to the index, and it will be appended to the object. Lastly, add the data to the map again:

```
heatmapLayer.addData(myData.data);
```

> If you do not use an index, you will overwrite the data with the one item you were trying to add.

Creating an interactive heatmap

A heatmap is an alternative visualization to a point map. A point map often becomes cluttered with large markers that make it hard to find hotspots. In an intensity heatmap, a single point could be a hotspot. The color coding of values in a heatmap makes it easy to see patterns in the data. Heatmaps can also be used to visualize other spatial data, such as tracking where a mouse moves on a web page or where a person's eyes travel when reading something on the screen. In this example, you will learn how to create a heatmap that responds to user mouse clicks on the map:

1. First, include a reference to `Leaflet.heat.js`:

    ```
    <script src="Leaflet-heat.js"></script>
    ```

2. Next, disable the `doubleClickZoom` option on the map. Since the user will be clicking on the map to make the heatmap, you need to do this so that when the user clicks too fast, which they will, the map does not zoom:

    ```
    var map = L.map("map",{doubleClickZoom:false}).setView([35.10418, -106.62987], 10);
    ```

3. Create a blank dataset that can be added to the map. This allows the user to draw on a fresh canvas:

    ```
    var points=[];
    ```

4. Add the data to the map:

    ```
    var heat = L.heatLayer(points,{maxZoom:10}).addTo(map);
    ```

5. Create a function to handle the user clicks. This function will add points to the layer by catching the latitude and longitude of the mouse click. The `e` parameter is an event object that is automatically sent on the map click. The object contains information about the event and, in this example, you take the latitude and longitude, as shown in the following code:

```
Function addpoint(e){
heat.addLatLng(e.latlng);
}
```

6. Connect the function to an event, in this case, `click`:

```
map.on('click',addpoint);
```

Your map, after clicking several times, should look like what is shown in the following screenshot:

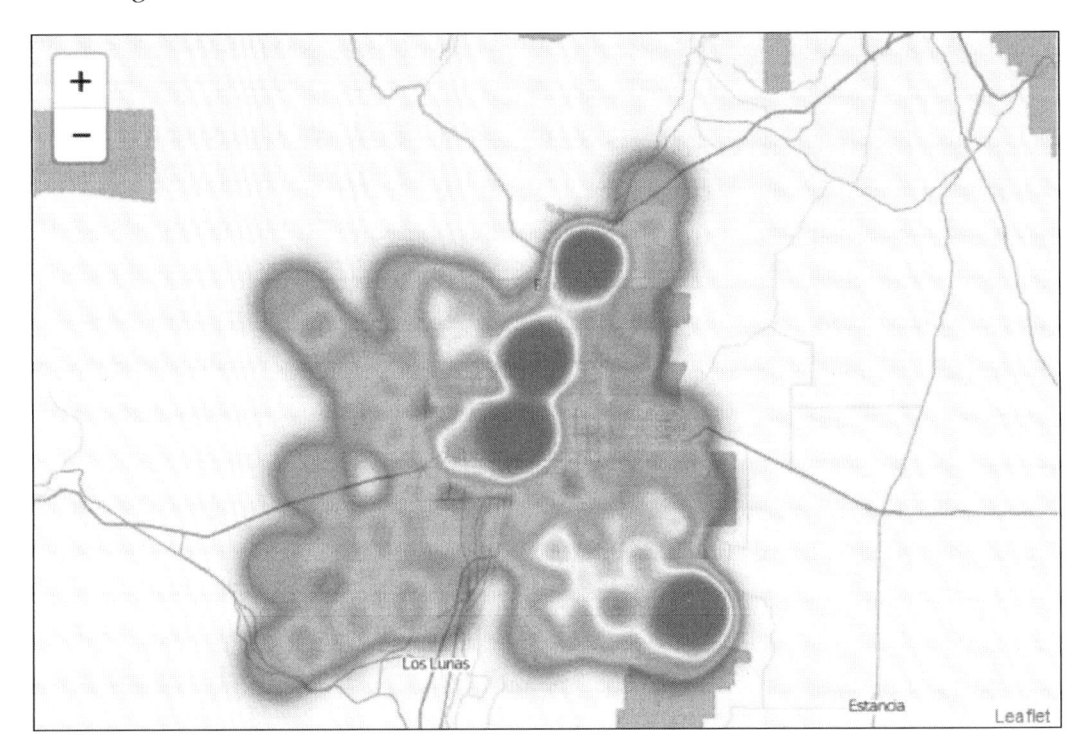

Animating a heatmap

So far, you have created a heatmap that showed you the current density of points and intensities, but what if you wanted to show a heatmap that changed over time? In this last example, you will learn how to create a heatmap animation.

An animated heatmap is not as complicated as it might sound. Animation is nothing more than adding and removing data from the map, and you have covered these skills earlier in the chapter. The trick to this example is in the organization of your data and taking advantage of timing events in JavaScript. The following steps will walk you through making an animated heatmap:

1. Reference the heatmap plugin:

   ```
   <script src="Leaflet-heat.js"></script>
   ```

2. Next, separate your data into an array per time period. Name your data with the same name, plus a number that increments the number based on the time period. The following code can be used for this purpose:

   ```
   var points1=[[35,-106],[35,-106]];
   var points2=[[35.10418, -106.62987],[32,-104]];
   var points4=[[33, -104.],[35,-107]];
   ```

3. Add a starting dataset to the map:

   ```
   var heat = L.heatLayer(points1,{maxZoom:10}).addTo(map);
   ```

4. Next, create a variable that will iterate through the datasets and a string that holds the name of the datasets. Note that the iterator starts at 2. This is because you loaded `points1` before the loop:

   ```
   x=2;
   var name="";
   ```

5. Create an interval and pass a function and the time in milliseconds (1,000 milliseconds are equal to one second):

   ```
   var interval = setInterval(function(){run()},1000);
   ```

Creating Heatmaps and Choropleth Maps

6. Create the function that will perform the animation. The following code creates a `name` string, that is, the data name concatenated with the iteration number. The current layer is removed from the map and the next layer is added. You cannot call a variable using a string as its name, so we use `window[name]`. Lastly, the code increments the x iterator:

```
function run(){
name="points"+x.toString();
map.removeLayer(heat);
heat = L.heatLayer(window[name],{maxZoom:10}).addTo(map);
var x++;
}
```

When you load the map, you should see the first dataset:

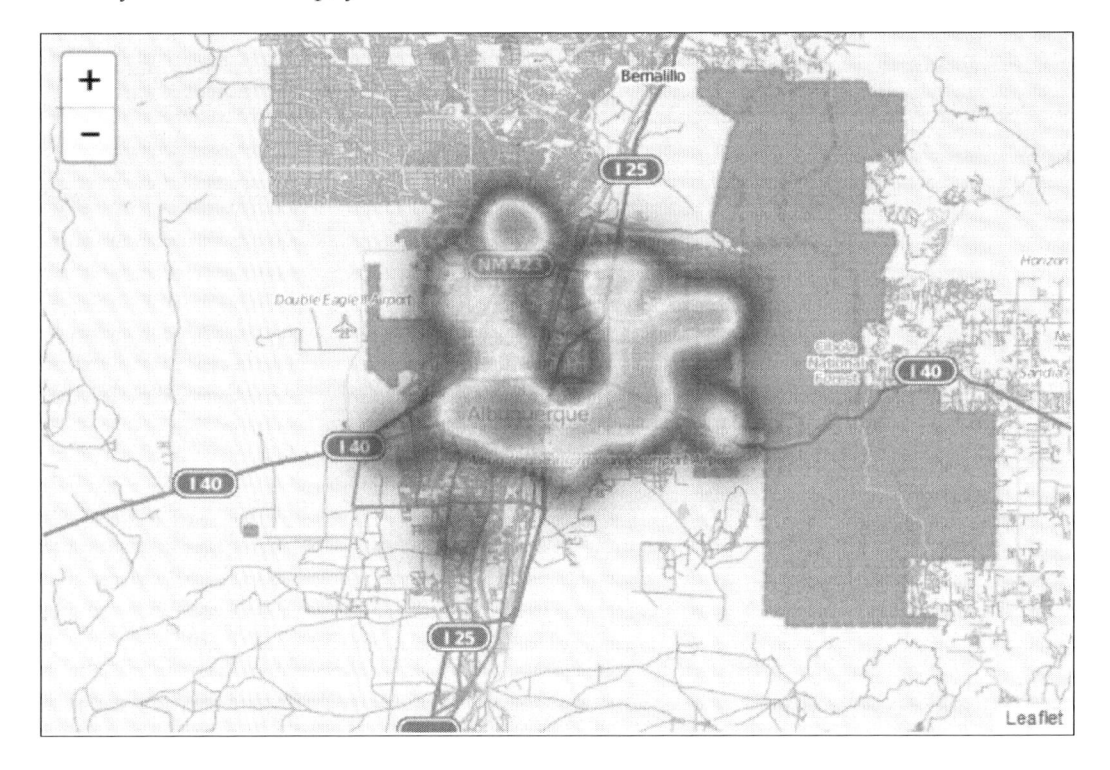

Then, the data will change every second. The following screenshot shows you what the map will look like after a few seconds:

Creating a choropleth map with Leaflet

In the previous examples, you used heatmaps to color code a map based on the density or intensity of points. A choropleth map also measures the intensity or density of a statistical variable but within polygons. A popular choropleth map is the population density by county. Choropleth maps do not require any plugins, as was the case with the heatmap examples. A choropleth map is usually created by styling GeoJSON based on a property.

The GeoJSON data

When adding a large amount of GeoJSON data to a map, it is easier to place the code in a separate JavaScript file. This clears your HTML file of hundreds of lines of code, which makes it hard to focus on building the map. When you place the GeoJSON code in a JavaScript file, you will declare it as a variable, as shown in the following code:

```
var ct = {"type": "FeatureCollection", "features": [{"geometry":
{"type": "Polygon", "coordinates": [[[-106.501132, 35.093911], [-
106.501231, 35.09385], [-106.501481, 35.09376], [-106.50201,
35.09371], [-106.50344, 35.093728], [-106.50424, 35.093709], [-
106.50574, 35.093706], [-106.50634, 35.093748], [-106.50748,
35.09368], [-106.508548, 35.0937], [-106.50984, 35.093646], [-
106.51071, 35.093618], [-106.51177, 35.093641], [-106.51295,
35.093613], [-106.513934, 35.09361], [-106.51528, 35.093581], [-
106.51533, 35.09648], [-106.51534, 35.096889], [-106.515398,
35.09966], [-106.515437, 35.101462], [-106.51419, 35.101452], [-
106.51366, 35.10143], [-106.51334, 35.10141], [-106.51308,
35.1014], [-106.51198, 35.101329], [-106.5109, 35.1013], [-
106.50975, 35.10123], [-106.50872, 35.10119], [-106.50641,
35.101106], [-106.50643, 35.101358], [-106.50441, 35.101237], [-
106.50362, 35.10119], [-106.50289, 35.101146], [-106.50187,
35.101085], [-106.50083, 35.10101], [-106.50058, 35.100989], [-
106.50021, 35.10096], [-106.49947, 35.100954], [-106.499153,
35.100933], [-106.49887, 35.100905], [-106.49849, 35.100892], [-
106.497853, 35.100895], [-106.49745, 35.10086], [-106.497415,
35.10086], [-106.49766, 35.094788], [-106.49881, 35.09483], [-
106.49947, 35.09487], [-106.49977, 35.09498], [-106.50022,
35.095099], [-106.5007, 35.094291], [-106.50093, 35.094034], [-
106.501132, 35.093911]]]}, "type": "Feature", "properties":
{"NAME10": "1.26", "AWATER10": 0.0, "TRACTCE10": "000126",
"ALAND10": 1315885.0, "INTPTLAT10": "+35.0975423", "FUNCSTAT10":
"S", "observed": "", "NAMELSAD10": "Census Tract 1.26",
"COUNTYFP10": "001", "STATEFP10": "35", "MTFCC10": "G5020",
"GEOID10": "35001000126", "id": 6059554, "INTPTLON10": "-
106.5067917"}}]};
```

The preceding code is for a single feature. The complete file contains 153 features. This would add over fifty 8.5" x 11" pages to your HTML file. Notice that the file is not GeoJSON but JavaScript. It is a variable declaration. When you reference this file in your HTML, you can call the `ct` variable in your script. Once you have your data as a variable in a JavaScript file, link to it in `LeafletEssentials.html`:

```
<script src="censustracts.js"></script>
```

The preceding code shows how you have referenced any included JavaScript file.

Setting the color with a function

The next step in making a choropleth map is to give each feature a color based on the statistical variable you are mapping. Define a function to handle the ranges of values, as shown in the following code:

```
function color(x) {
return x > 200000 ? '#990000' :
x> 100000  ? '#d7301f' :
x> 30000   ? '#ef6548' :
x> 20000   ? '#fc8d59' :
x> 10000   ? '#fdbb84' :
x> 5000    ? '#fdd49e' :
x> 0       ? '#fee8c8' :'#fff7ec';
          }
```

The preceding code takes a parameter and measures a value, returning the color. Darker colors are returned for higher values. It is always best to stick to a standard coloring progression. Using a single hue progression—a single color from light to dark—should serve you well. Using a tool such as Color Brewer will help ensure that you use a good color scheme. You can find it at http://colorbrewer2.org/. This will provide you with color values in RGB, CMYK, and HEX.

Styling the GeoJSON data

Next, you need to create a function to style the GeoJSON data. Using a function allows you to style each individual feature based on a property. The following code will style the features:

```
Function myStyle(feature) {
return {
fillColor: color(feature.properties.AWATER10),
weight: 1,
opacity: 1,
     color: 'white',
     fillOpacity: 0.85
   };
}
```

The function takes the feature as a parameter and styles it using a few options. The important option is the `fillColor` option. This is where you call the `color()` function and pass the value of `AWATER10` for each feature. Lastly, add the `GeoJSONLayer` variable to the map and use the style function as a parameter, as shown in the following code:

```
var GeoJSONLayer = L.GeoJSON(ct, {style: myStyle}).addTo(map);
```

The preceding code adds the layer to the map using the style function. The result will look like what is shown in the following screenshot:

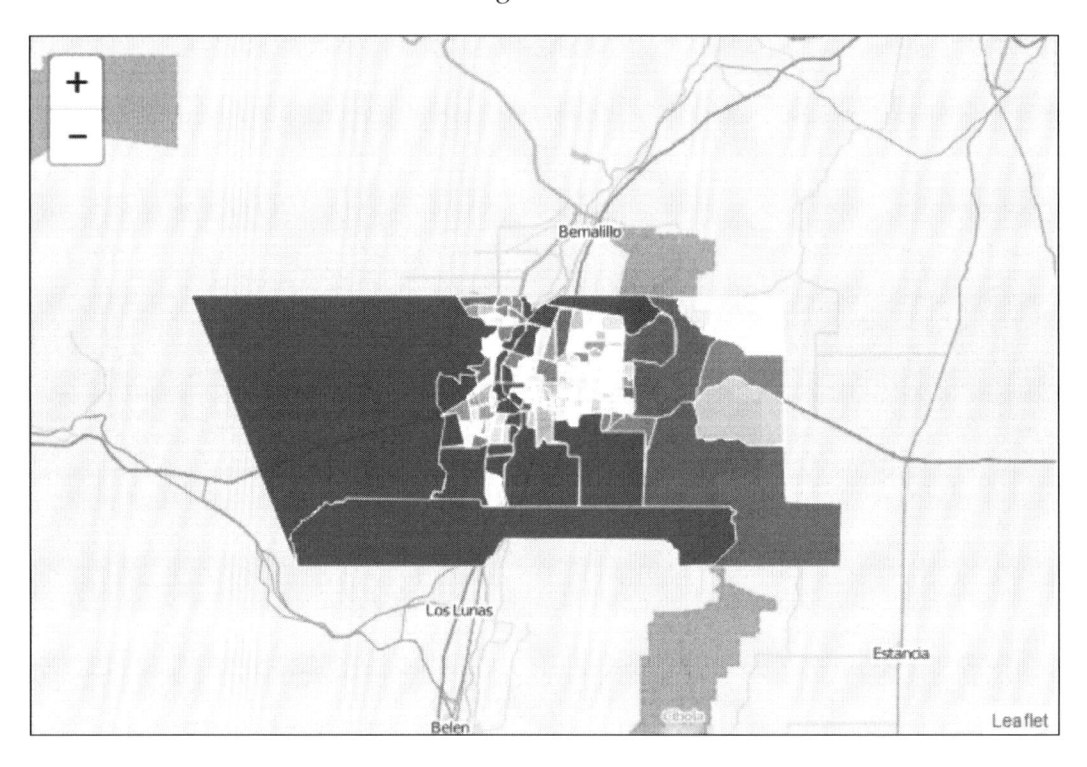

Using a total value, such as the area of water in a census tract, can be improved upon by normalizing your data using the land area. This is important because without normalization, values can be skewed. For example, assume two locations with a land area of 100 acres and 50 acres, respectively. If they both have a lake that is 10 acres, and you color code with normalization, they will be of the same color. When you normalize, the values will be `.1` and `.2`. The second location is 20 percent water and the first is only 10 percent. This fact is lost without normalization. In the next example, you will build a map that shows the difference between total and normalized values.

Creating a normalized choropleth map

In this example, you will create a choropleth map that displays both the total area and the total area divided by the total land area. The following steps will walk you through this:

1. Using the code from the previous example, add another color function with values for the new ranges. They will be much smaller values than values for the total:

   ```
   function densitycolor(x) {
   return x > 0.15 ? '#990000' :
   x> 0.12   ? '#d7301f' :
   x> 0.06   ? '#ef6548' :
   x> 0.03   ? '#fc8d59' :
   x> 0.01   ? '#fdbb84' :
   x> 0.005  ? '#fdd49e' :
   x> 0     ? '#fee8c8' :'#fff7ec';
   }
   ```

2. Next, define another style function. The key difference in this function is that the value passed to the color function will be `water/land`:

   ```
   function densityStyle(feature) {
   return {
   fillColor:
   densitycolor(feature.properties.AWATER10/feature.properties
   .ALAND10),
   weight: 1,
   opacity: 1,
       color: 'white',
       fillOpacity: 1
      };
   }
   ```

3. Create two buttons on the bottom of the map to select which choropleth map is to be displayed. Connect the buttons to a function:

   ```
   <button onclick="total()">Total</button>
   <button onclick="density()">Water/Land</button>
   ```

Creating Heatmaps and Choropleth Maps

4. Lastly, write the functions that display the layers. Remove the other layer after you display the correct layer:

```
function total(){
var GeoJSONLayer = L.GeoJSON(ct, {style:
myStyle}).addTo(map);
removeLayer(densitylayer);
}
function density(){
var densitylayer=L.GeoJSON(ct,GeoJSON {style:
densityStyle}).addTo(map);
removeLayer(GeoJSONLayer);
}
```

Your completed map should be blank. You did not load a layer on the map. You can now select which layer you want to see by clicking on one of the buttons on the bottom of the map. Try clicking on the other button. Click on the button labeled **Water/Land**. Your map should look like what is shown in the following screenshot:

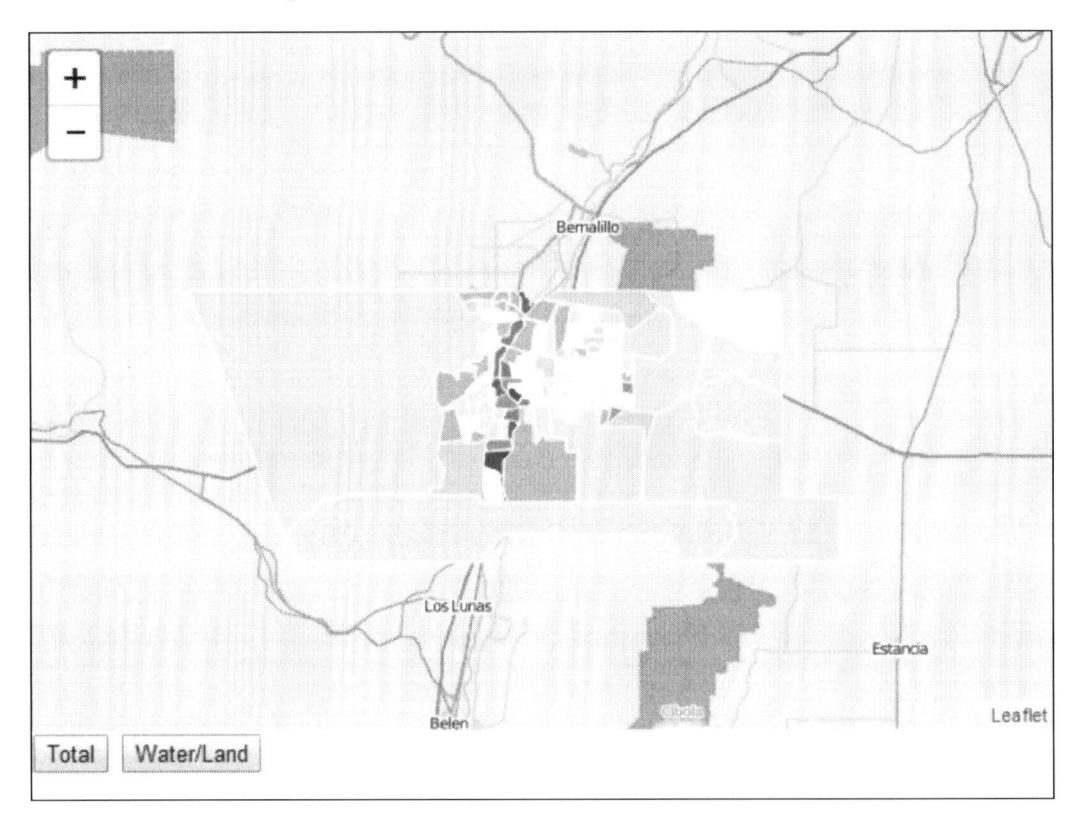

Notice that once you normalize the land area, the areas with the most water—darkest red—are the small tracts near the **Rio Grande** area. These large tracts of land have water, but this makes up a small percent of the total area.

Summary

In this chapter, you have taken your map-making skills beyond points, lines, polygons, and GeoJSON to create map visualizations—heatmaps and choropleth maps. You have learned how to use two different plugins to make heatmaps and how to style them for maximum visual effect. You also learned how to make your heatmap interactive and create animations to show the time series data. Choropleth maps did not require plugins. You learned how to style GeoJSON data to make a choropleth map. Lastly, you learned the difference between totals and normalized data.

In the next chapter, you will learn how to create your own markers. You will also learn about several plugins that animate and enhance the markers on your map.

4
Creating Custom Markers

In *Chapter 3, Creating Heatmaps and Choropleth Maps*, you learned how to style your maps to create a heatmap and a choropleth map. Leaflet allows you to further customize the style of your map by modifying the default markers. In this chapter, you will learn how to style markers by creating custom marker icons. You will also learn about the available marker plugins for styles and effects.

Creating a custom marker

In Leaflet, a marker is made from two images: an image that represents the marker and a second image that serves as the shadow to create depth. When you download Leaflet, there is an `images` folder. This folder contains the default marker: the blue pin that you have seen in your maps and a small shadow image. The images are named `marker-icon.png` and `marker-shadow.png`. The default marker and shadow are shown in the following screenshots:

Creating Custom Markers

Preparing your workspace in GIMP

To create your own custom marker, you will need to draw an image in a painting application. In this example, you will use the free **GNU Image Manipulation Program** (**GIMP**). GIMP is a powerful imaging program that is similar to Adobe Photoshop which runs on most operating systems and is completely free.
To download GIMP, go to `http://www.gimp.org/downloads/` and click on **Download GIMP 2.8.10**.

> You do not need to select a 32- or 64-bit version. GIMP includes both and will determine the appropriate version when the installer runs.

Once GIMP is installed, launch the application. The application contains three windows: two panels on the left- and right-hand side of the screen and the main window in the center. You can combine the three windows into a standard single window application by navigating to **Windows | Single-Window Mode**. To create a new image file, navigate to **File | New...**. You will be prompted with a new image dialog box. Enter a width and height for the icon image. If the advanced options are not expanded, click on the menu to expand the window. You can enter a resolution or accept the default. The **Fill with** option is the most important. You must select **Transparency** from the dropdown. If you do not select **Transparency**, your icon will be a square or rectangle with a background color. This will not look flattering on your map. The dialog box should now look like the following screenshot:

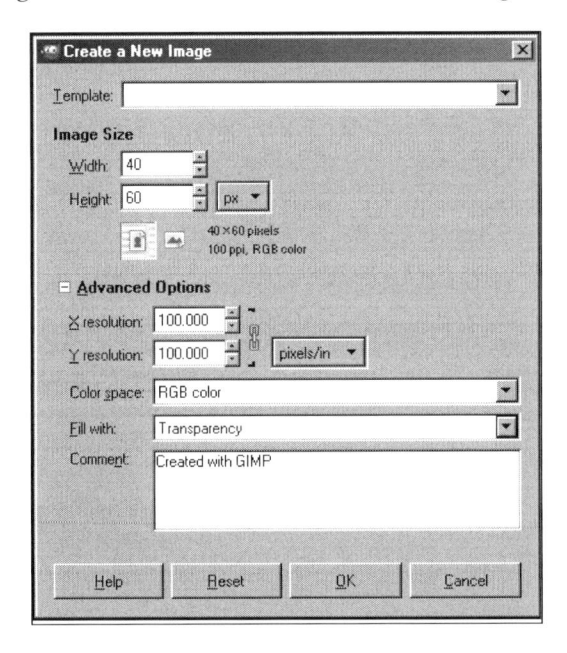

[78]

Drawing and saving your image

Now that the canvas is set up, you can draw your image. How we draw the image is beyond the scope of this book.

> If you would like to learn about GIMP, check out *Gimp 2.6 Cookbook*, *Juan Manuel Ferreyra*, *Packt Publishing*, available at `http://www.packtpub.com/gimp-2-6-cookbook/book`.

If you are comfortable drawing in GIMP, create an image that can be used as your icon. Once you have created the image, navigate to **File | Export As...**. If you try to use the **Save** or **Save As...** options, you will not get the options for PNG. The **Export Image** dialog box allows you to choose the filename and where you would like to save the file. On the bottom-left corner of the dialog, expand the menu labeled **Select File Type (By Extension)**. Scroll down to **PNG image** and click on **Export**. You will be prompted with the **Export Image as PNG** dialog box. You must check the **Save color values from transparent pixels** option. The options form should look like the one shown in the following screenshot:

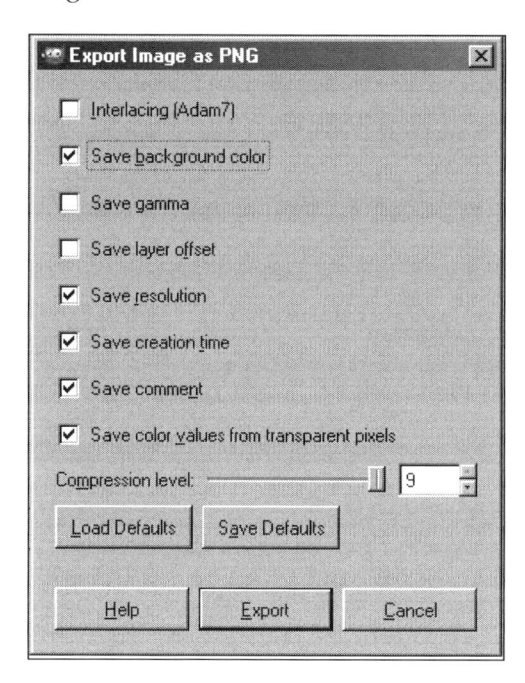

Click on the **Export** button to save the image. The following screenshot is the finished icon:

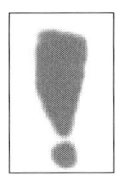

Drawing the marker shadow

Create another new image in GIMP, but select a larger width and smaller height: 60 x 40. The shadow will need to start at the same point as the tip of the marker and extend at approximately 45 degrees to the right. In GIMP, you can move the cursor over the image and see the pixel coordinates of the cursor. The shadow image is drawn horizontally at 20 pixels. The image in the following screenshot shows you the cursor at the tip of the icon and the coordinates in the lower-left corner of the window:

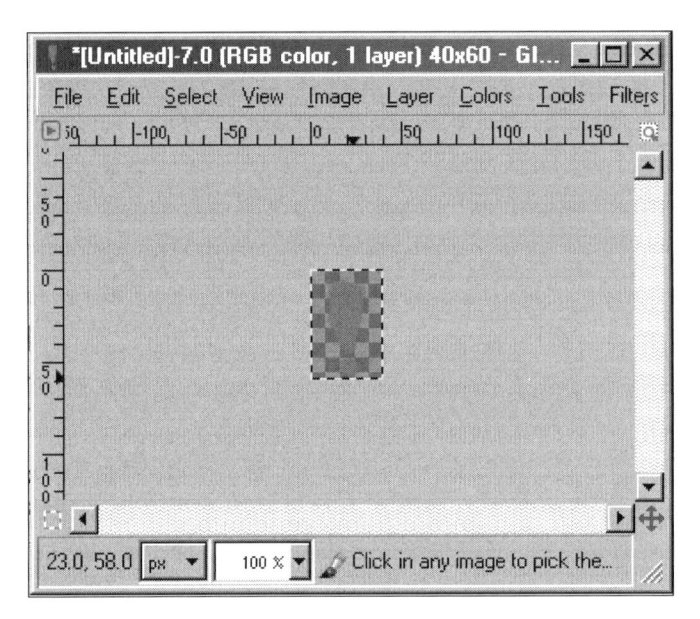

On the shadow image, start shading from pixel 20 towards the upper-right corner of the image. The finished shadow image will look something like what is shown in the following screenshot:

Using an image as an icon

You can also use an image as an icon. The image need not be PNG or have a transparent background. You can correct all of these things in GIMP. In GIMP, navigate to **File** | **Open** and select your image. The image in this example is JPG with a white background.

In the **Layers** panel, you should see a single layer with a picture of your image on it. Right-click on the layer and select **Add Alpha Channel**.

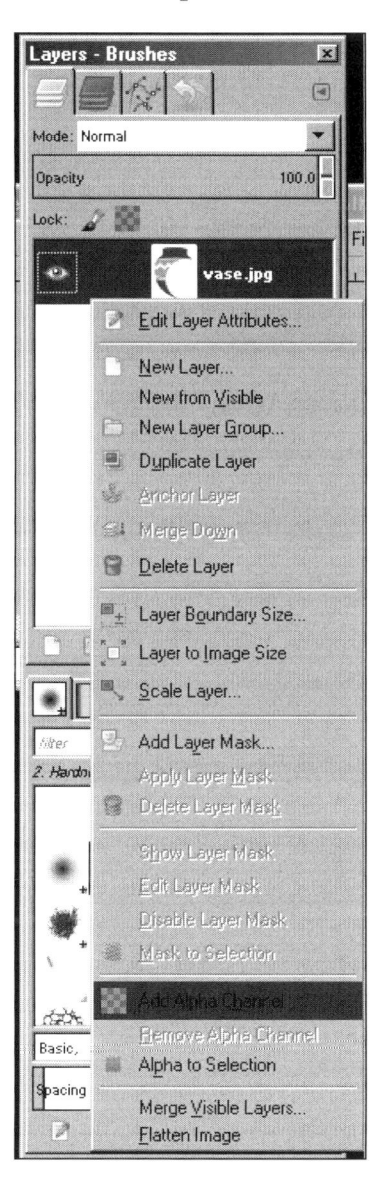

You can now select the erase tool or the magic wand and remove the background color. Export the image as instructed in the previous section. You will still need to draw a shadow for your marker icon. Follow the same steps as the shadow in the previous example and save the image.

Now that you have two images—the icon and the shadow—it is time to use them in your Leaflet map.

Using a custom marker in Leaflet

To create a marker icon in Leaflet, you need to create an instance of the `L.icon` class. The `L.icon` class takes 10 options, as follows:

- iconUrl
- iconRetinaUrl
- iconSize
- iconAnchor
- shadowUrl
- shadowRetinaUrl
- shadowSize
- shadowAnchor
- popupAnchor
- className

The only required option is `iconUrl`. In this example, you will ignore the retina images and the class name. Open `LeafletEssentials.html` and add the following code:

```
var myIcon = L.icon({
    iconUrl: 'mymarker.png',
    shadowUrl: 'shadow.png',
    iconSize:      [40, 60],
    shadowSize:    [60, 40],
    iconAnchor:    [20, 60],
    shadowAnchor: [20, 40],
    popupAnchor:   [0, -53]
});
```

The preceding code sets the options. The `iconUrl` option directs the URL to the icon image and the `shadowUrl` option directs the URL to the shadow image. The `iconSize` and `shadowSize` options require the dimensions of the images in the format of width by height.

The `iconAnchor` options set the point at which the marker and icon touch the map and where the pop up touches the icon. The marker had a point at the horizontal pixel 20, so this will be the anchor plus the height of the image in pixels. The shadow was drawn at the point of the marker, so its anchor will be at 20 and its height will be 40 pixels. You want the pop up to be drawn at the top in the center of the marker, so you must set its anchor accordingly.

The `popupAnchor` option is set relative to the `iconAnchor` option. The icon point is centered horizontally, so the pop-up anchor will be 0 pixels, making it anchored at 20. To place the anchor at the top of the marker, you subtract pixels. Choosing a value of -53 for the pop-up anchor opens the pop up just above the icon.

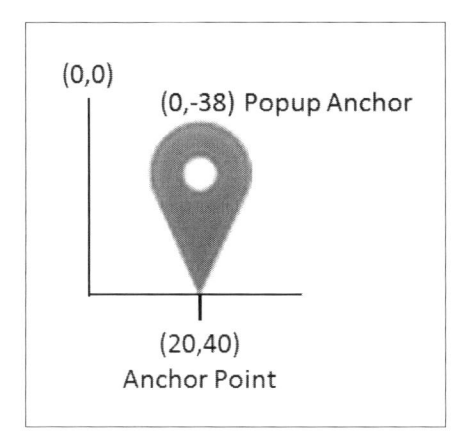

Next, you need to create a marker and tell it to use your new icon. The following code will do just that:

```
var marker = L.marker([35.10418, -106.62987],{icon:
myIcon}).addTo(map).bindPopup("I am a custom marker.");
```

In *Chapter 1, Creating Maps with Leaflet,* you created markers with several options—one being `draggable:true`. The marker class also takes an icon as an option. In the preceding code, the `icon` option takes the name of an `L.Icon` object.

Creating Custom Markers

Save `LeafletEssentials.html` and open it in your browser. You should see a map similar to the one shown in the following screenshot:

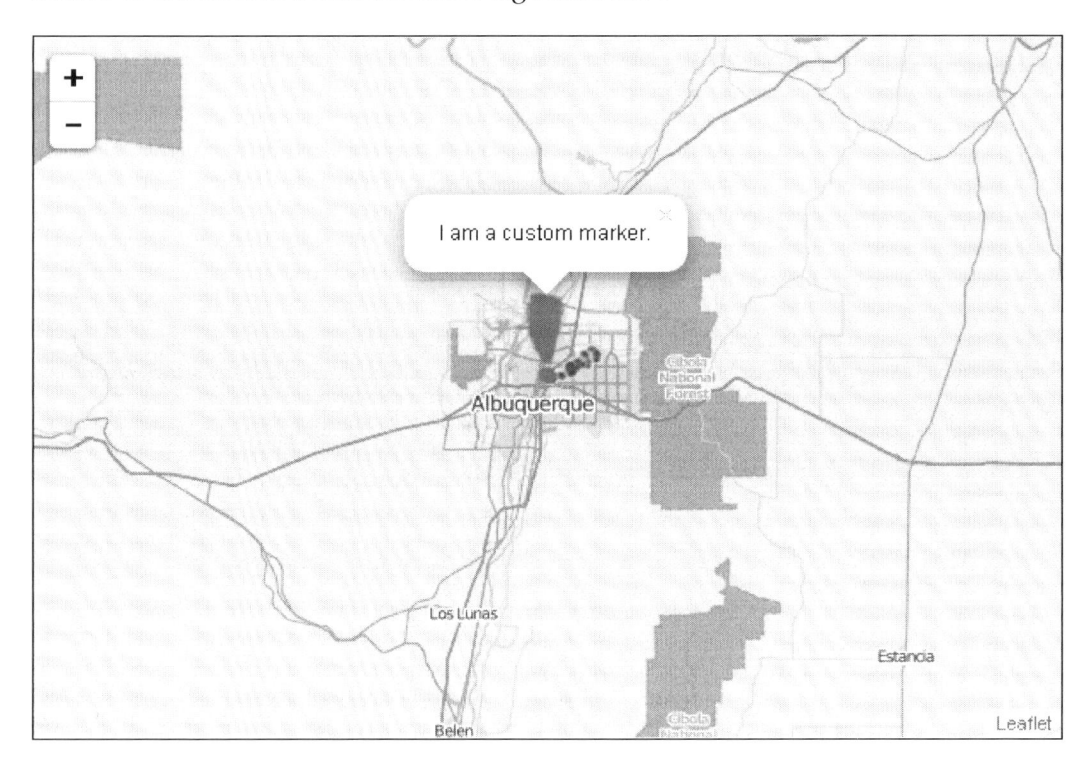

Defining an L.Icon class

You can also extend the `L.Icon` class to create your own marker class. This allows you to create markers in a variety of colors and only specify the size and anchor options once. This example will look very similar to the previous example. Add the following code to your `LeafletEssentials.html` file:

```
var MyIcon = L.Icon.extend({
    options:{
    shadowUrl: 'shadow.png',
    iconSize:     [40, 60],
    shadowSize:   [60, 40],
    iconAnchor:   [20, 60],
    shadowAnchor: [20, 40],
    popupAnchor:  [0, -53] }
});
```

The preceding code looks almost identical to the code in the previous example, except for the following differences:

- The first line, which instead of creating a new `L.icon` class, extends it
- The options are wrapped in an object in line two
- There is no `iconUrl` option

By wrapping the options in an object, you can pass additional options when you create the marker. Add the following code to the `LeafletEssentials.html` file:

```
var redIcon= new myIcon({iconUrl: 'mymarker.png'});
var blueIcon=new myIcon({iconUrl: 'mybluemarker.png'});
```

The preceding code sets the `iconUrl` option for each new `icon` object. Now, in one line of code, you have a red and blue icon. You can now assign the icon to a marker, as shown in the following code:

```
var marker = L.marker([35.10418, -106.62987],{icon:
redIcon}).addTo(map).bindPopup("I am a custom marker.");
var marker = L.marker([35, -106],{icon:
blueIcon}).addTo(map).bindPopup("I am a custom marker.");
```

In the preceding code, each marker is assigned a different color icon. The result is shown in the following screenshot:

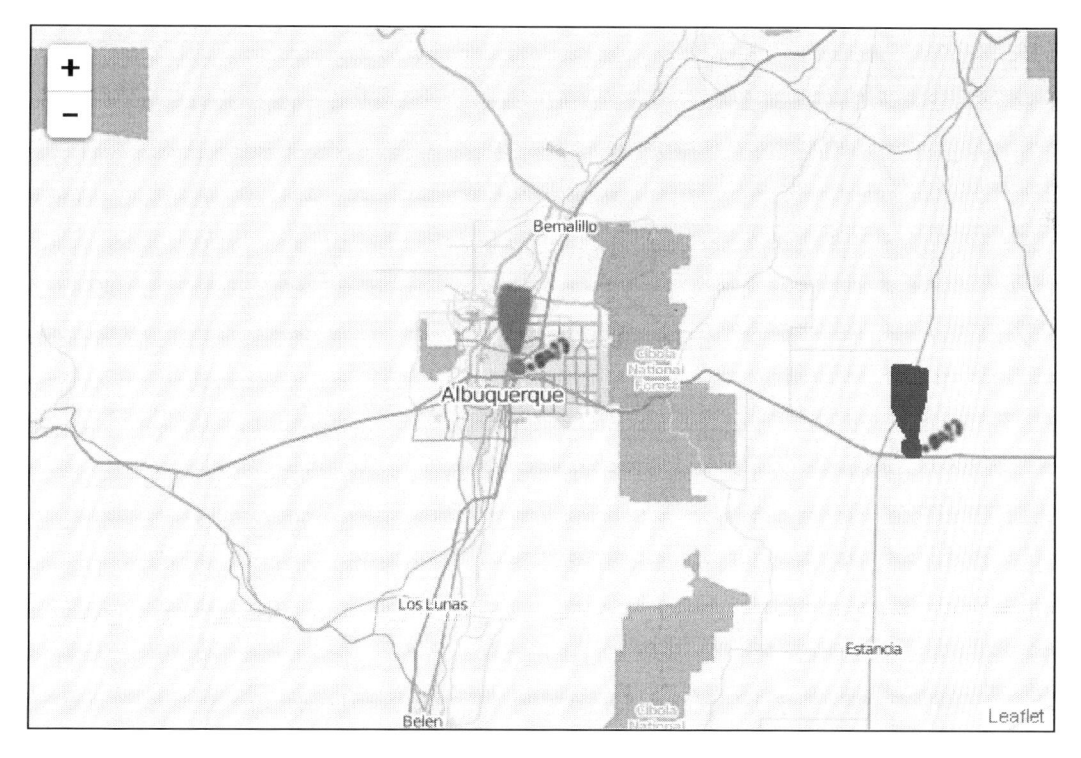

Creating Custom Markers

Using predefined markers with plugins

In the first three chapters, you used the default Leaflet marker. In this chapter, you have just learned how to draw your own or use a pre-existing image. Rolling your own is not always practical, especially if you are not proficient in drawing. In this section, you will learn about two plugins that have stylish markers that you can customize and use in your Leaflet map: Maki markers and Bootstrap/Awesome markers.

Using Mapbox Maki markers

Mapbox is a company that provides a mapping platform and tools. Its icons have been made available through the `Leaflet.Makimarkers` plugin. You can download the plugin at `https://github.com/jseppi/Leaflet.MakiMarkers`.

> You can learn about Mapbox by visiting their website at `http://mapbox.com`.

Maki markers is an open source icon library with over 100 available markers. You can find a full list of their names in the `Leaflet.MakiMarkers.js` file or go to the website at `https://www.mapbox.com/maki/`. The following screenshot shows you all of the icons:

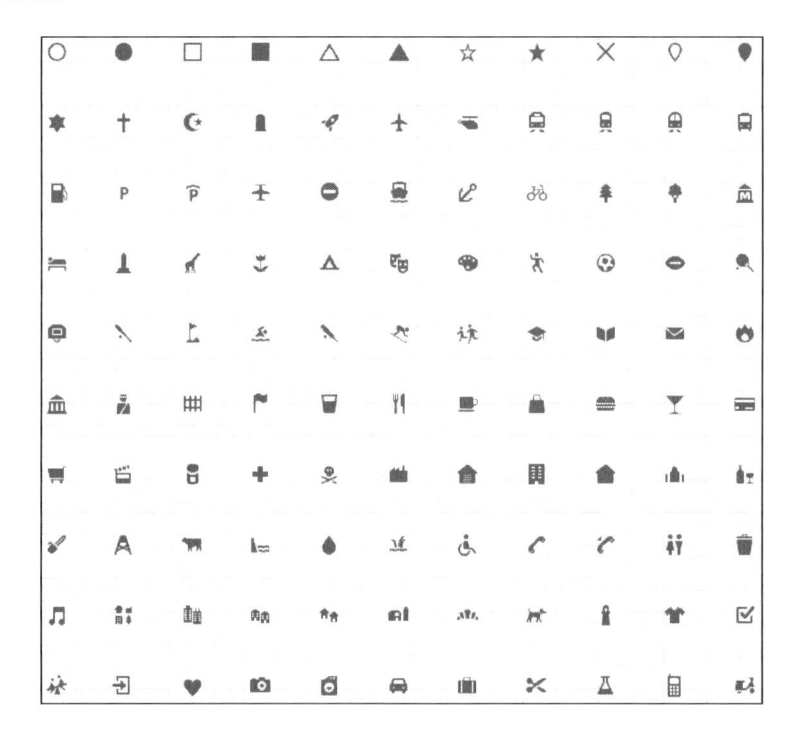

The icons in the preceding screenshot are placed on a colored marker symbol. Using the markers in your map requires only two lines of code and three options. The following steps will help you create a Maki marker and place it on your map:

1. Add a reference to the JavaScript file. No CSS file is required with this plugin:

   ```
   <script src="Leaflet.MakiMarkers.js"></script>
   ```

2. Create an icon. You have to choose three options: the icon image you want to use, the hex color value of the marker, and the size (s, m, l):

   ```
   var icon = L.MakiMarkers.icon({icon: "rocket", color: "#0a0", size: "l"});
   ```

3. Add the icon to a marker and add the marker to the map:

   ```
   L.marker([35.10418, -106.62987], {icon: icon}).addTo(map);
   ```

When you select a color, there will be an outline in a lighter shade of the same color. The following screenshot shows you the results of the preceding code:

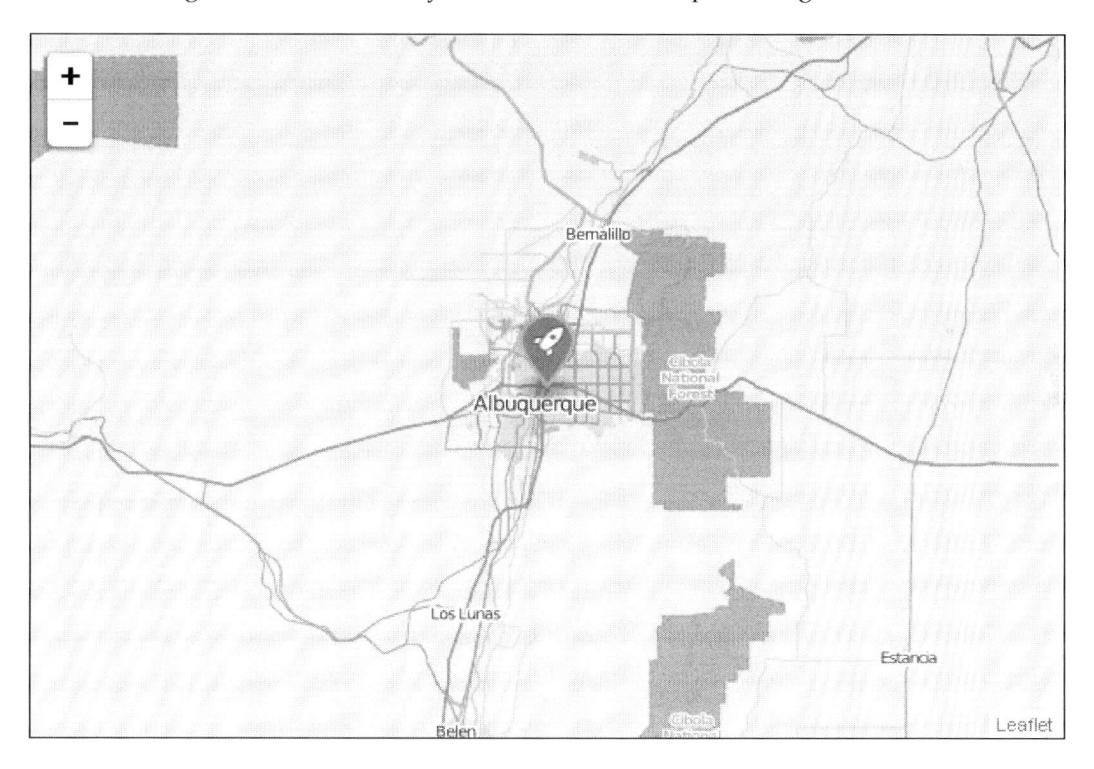

[87]

Using Bootstrap and Font Awesome markers

Another plugin for Leaflet that allows you to use predefined markers is `Leaflet.awesome.markers`. This plugin allows you to choose the Twitter Bootstrap markers or the Font Awesome markers. If you can't choose, you can always use both. The different libraries provide different icons to your markers and slightly different functionalities. Which one you use is a personal preference. You can download the plugin at `https://github.com/lvoogdt/Leaflet.awesome-markers`.

Using `Leaflet.awesome.markers` is almost the same procedure as you used in the Maki marker example. You can perform the following steps:

1. Add a reference to Twitter Bootstrap or Font Awesome or both. Also, add a reference to the CSS and JavaScript for `Leaflet.awesome.markers`:

   ```
   <link rel="stylesheet" href="http://netdna.bootstrapcdn.com/bootstrap/3.2.0/css/bootstrap.min.css">
   <link rel="stylesheet" href="http://netdna.bootstrapcdn.com/bootstrap/3.2.0/css/bootstrap-theme.min.css">
   <link href="http://maxcdn.bootstrapcdn.com/font-awesome/4.1.0/css/font-awesome.min.css" rel="stylesheet">
   <link rel="stylesheet" href="Leaflet.awesome-markers.css">
   <script src="http://netdna.bootstrapcdn.com/bootstrap/3.2.0/js/bootstrap.min.js"></script>
   <script src="Leaflet.awesome-markers.js"></script>
   ```

2. Create a Twitter Bootstrap marker and add it to the map. The Bootstrap marker is the default. You only need to set the icon image and color options. Create the marker and add it to the map:

   ```
   var redMarker = L.AwesomeMarkers.icon({
       icon: 'tint',
       markerColor: 'red'
   });
     L.marker([35.10418, -106.62987], {icon: redMarker}).addTo(map);
   ```

Chapter 4

3. Create a Font Awesome marker and add it to the map. Since Bootstrap is the default, you need to use the `prefix` option with the value of `fa` for Font Awesome. This example also uses the `spin:true` option to create an animated spinning marker. Create the marker and add it to the map:

```
var blueMarker = L.AwesomeMarkers.icon({
    prefix:'fa',
    spin:true,
    icon: 'spinner',
    markerColor: 'blue'
});
L.marker([35, -106], {icon: blueMarker}).addTo(map);
```

The preceding code will produce the map shown in the following screenshot:

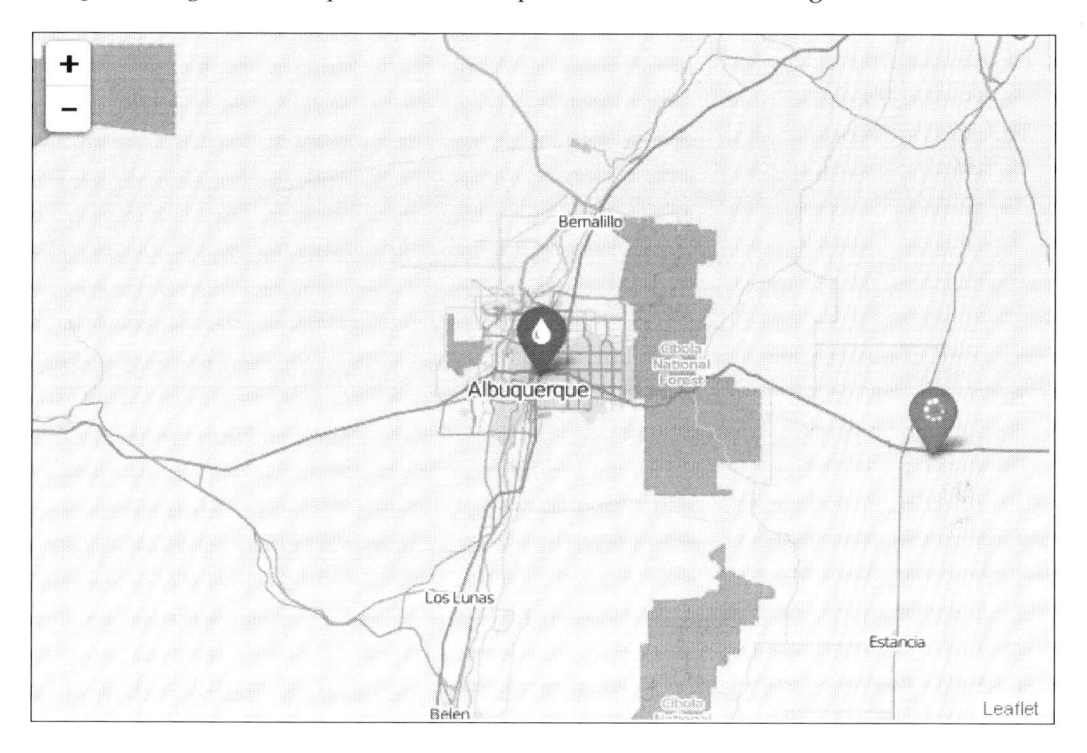

You might not always have the time to create your own markers, and when you have the option to use icons by Mapbox, Twitter, or Font Awesome, why reinvent the wheel? Take advantage of what has already been done, and do it extremely well.

Clustering markers with Leaflet.markercluster

As you create more maps, you will eventually run in to a dataset that is thousands of points. Displaying 10,000 points on a map results in a slow load time, lagging animation on zooming and panning, and makes it hard for the user to select a single marker or to make sense of the data. Clustering allows you to group markers into clusters—single points that expand as the zoom level increases. This way, you can get a sense of the magnitude of data without being visually overwhelmed by the sheer number of points. If you need to see a single point, you can zoom in to the region or point of interest. Leaflet.markercluster is a fast and powerful cluster implementation that is also visually appealing.

> You can download this plugin at https://github.com/Leaflet/Leaflet.markercluster.

Coding your first cluster map

A marker cluster is just another example of a layer in Leaflet. So, creating one should look very familiar to you. You need to perform the following steps:

1. Using LeafletEssentials.html, add a reference to the Leaflet.markercluster CSS files and the JS file, as shown in the following code:

    ```
    <link rel="stylesheet" href="MarkerCluster.Default.css" />
    <script src="Leaflet.markercluster.js"></script>
    ```

2. You can add a series of markers to the layer, but since you will be loading 723 points, you will use a JS file with the data inside. The data can have additional attributes. In this example, there is a link to an image file. Add a reference to the JS file that contains the data:

    ```
    <script src="art.js"></script>
    ```

3. Since you now know how to create custom marker icons, the following code creates an icon class and an icon that can be used when the clusters expand:

    ```
    var abqIcon = L.Icon.extend({
        options: {
            shadowUrl: 'vase-shadow.png',
            iconSize:    [50, 64],
            shadowSize:  [50, 64],
            iconAnchor:  [25, 64],
    ```

Chapter 4

```
            shadowAnchor: [0, 64],
            popupAnchor:  [-3, -64]
        }
    });

    var vase = new abqIcon({iconUrl: 'vase.png'});
```

4. Now, create a `markercluster` layer by creating an instance of the `MarkerClusterGroup` class. Set the `showCoverageOnHover` option to `false`:

   ```
   var markers = new
   L.MarkerClusterGroup({showCoverageOnHover:false});
   ```

5. To add markers to the group, you need a function that uses the array from the data file to loop through each data point and add the latitude, longitude, and any other attributes you want to use in the pop up to a marker. The loop creates a marker, binds a pop up, and adds the marker as a layer to the `markercluster` group. Then, call the function to start loading the data:

   ```
   function populate() {
     for (var i = 0; i < artPoints.length; i++) {
         var a = artPoints[i];
         var title = a[2];
   var marker = new L.Marker(new L.LatLng(a[0], a[1]), { icon:
   vase , title: title });
         marker.bindPopup(title);
         markers.addLayer(marker);

         }
     }

   populate();
   ```

6. Lastly, add the `markercluster` group layer to the map using the following code:

   ```
   map.addLayer(markers);
   ```

[91]

Creating Custom Markers

Your map should look like the following screenshot:

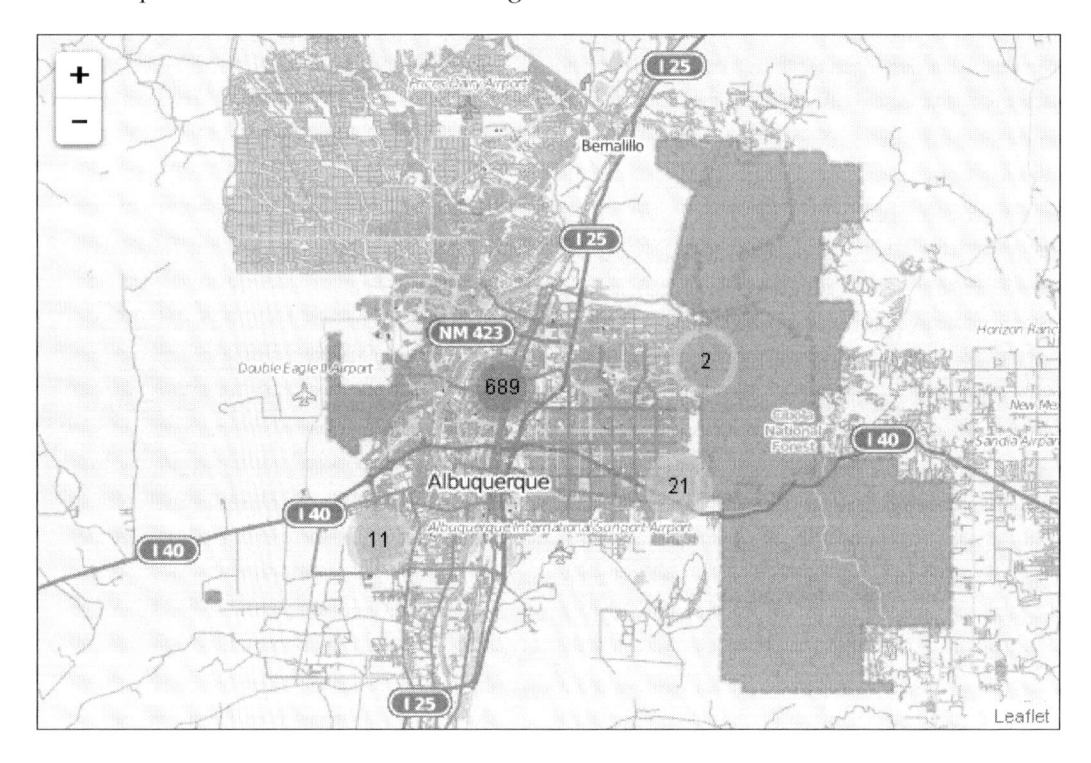

When you zoom in to the map, the clusters should expand and the groupings become smaller. They will then expand to reveal individual markers, as shown in the following screenshot:

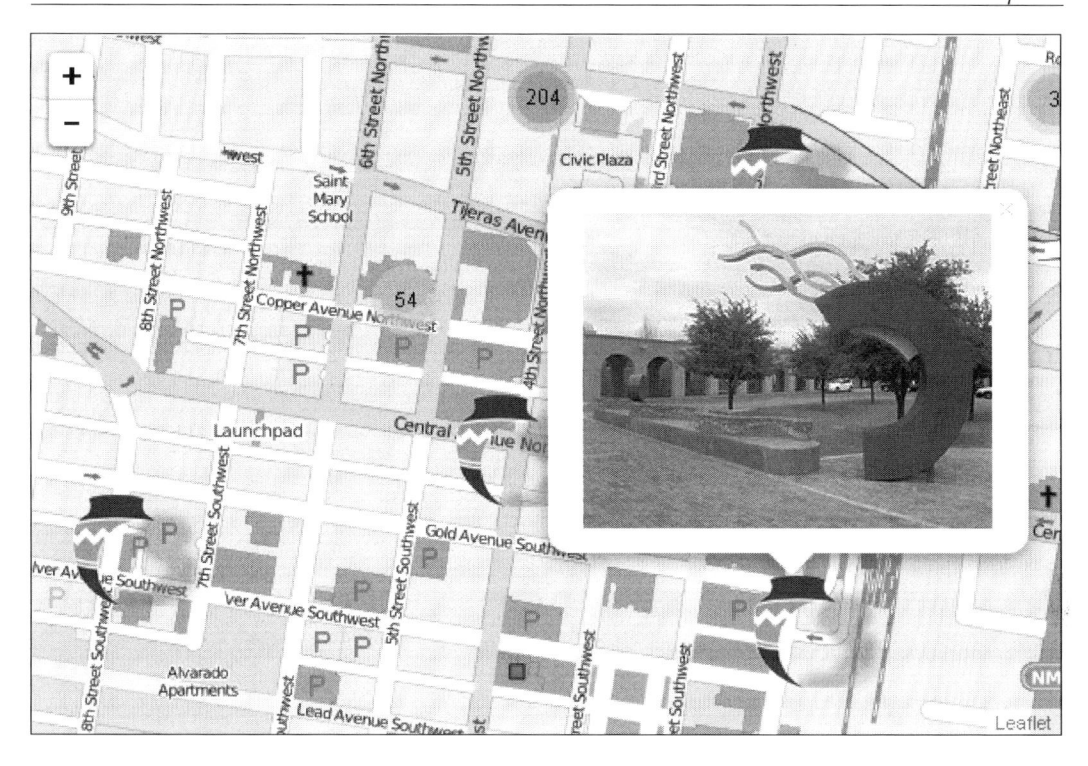

Methods and events available to markercluster layers

The `markercluster` layer has several options and methods that can be used to create and interact with your layer.

Options that default to true

There are four default options that are all set to `true`, as follows:

- showCoverageOnHover
- zoomToBoundsOnClick
- spiderfyOnMaxZoom
- removeOutsideVisibleBounds

The first option shows you a polygon that represents the coverage area of the markers in the cluster. This can be confusing as a colored polygon appears on the map. In the previous example, you set this option to `false`.

Creating Custom Markers

When you click on a cluster, the second option zooms to the polygon that represents the coverage area of the cluster you clicked on. When you zoom all the way into the map or use the defined `maxZoom` option, the cluster will expand to reveal the markers within it.

The last option improves performance by not displaying clusters that are not within a close proximity of the current map view. You do not need to see a cluster in New York if you are looking at Los Angeles.

Other options and events

The other options you might want to set are `animateAddingMarkers` and `maxClusterRadius`. Animated markers create a visually interesting map, but if you are using a large set of data points, it can slow the performance of your map. It is an effect that should be used sparingly and under the right conditions. Adjusting the radius of the cluster can create larger or smaller clusters. The default is 80 pixels. If you are displaying tightly grouped data, you will need a smaller number, and if you are displaying data that is dispersed, you might need a larger radius. In the previous example, if the radius is set to 5, the markers take over the map because they are not getting clustered due to the small radius. The following screenshot shows you the map when the radius is set to 5:

The preceding screenshot is cluttered with markers, making the map almost unreadable. The `markercluster` layer has events that you can subscribe to. Usually, you subscribe to an event on the map using `map.on(click, function)`. With the `markercluster` layer, you add a cluster to the available layer events so that they will apply to the `markercluster` layer, such as `markers.on(clusterclick,function)`.

Animating markers with plugins

In the next two sections, you will learn how to animate markers using the `Leaflet.BounceMarker` and `Leaflet.AnimatedMarker` plugins. Animation adds a wow factor to your map, but if overdone, it can make your map appear amateurish.

Bouncing your markers

The `Leaflet.BounceMarker` plugin does not have a large number of options to customize the markers or their behavior, but it provides a simple animation that is useful when you add markers to the map or on the hover event. You can download and learn more about the plugin at https://github.com/maximeh/leaflet.bouncemarker.

The following steps will show you how to add a bounce marker to your map:

1. Add a reference to the JavaScript file. There is no CSS file required for this plugin:

   ```
   <script src="bouncemarker.js"></script>
   ```

2. Creating a bounce marker is exactly the same as creating a standard Leaflet marker; the plugin adds an additional option to the `L.Marker` class. Because of this, the bounce marker has a `bounceOnAdd` option, and it defaults to `false`. Every marker you create will bounce unless you specify otherwise. Set this option to `true` for any markers you would like to bounce. Add the marker to the map.

   ```
   marker = new L.Marker([35.10418, -106.62987], {bounceOnAdd: true,}).addTo(map);
   ```

The only other options you can specify on a bounce marker are the height, duration, and a callback function when finished. You set them as shown in the following code:

```
marker.bounce({duration: 1000, height: 200}, function(){alert("Finished")});
```

Creating Custom Markers

Height is in pixels and duration is in milliseconds. Animation takes resources to run, so make sure that you do not create animations that run too quickly, or you will find that your marker disappears and only the shadow is visible. Also, remember that if you intend for your map to be consumed on mobile devices, the performance might be slower than on your desktop.

The `bounce()` method works well with the hover event. When there are many markers and they are tightly grouped, making the one you are hovering over bounce helps make sure that you click on the correct one.

To make a marker bounce on a hover event, subscribe to the event and call a function when the mouse hovers over the marker:

```
marker.on('mouseover',function(){marker.bounce({duration: 500, height: 100});});
```

The preceding code subscribes to the `mouseover` event and executes an anonymous function when the mouse hovers over the marker. The anonymous function calls the `bounce()` method, making the marker do just that when you move the mouse over it.

> The `Leaflet.BounceMarker` plugin is an excellent plugin; however, you might experience some hiccups in your animations. This is not to be blamed on the plugin, but rather on the nature of animations and the large number of resources they require.

Making your markers move

With the `Leaflet.AnimatedMarker` plugin, you can make your markers move along a polyline. This comes in handy when you want to draw attention to a route. A marker moving along the route attracts the eye more than a line on the map. For more information and to download the plugin, go to https://github.com/openplans/Leaflet.AnimatedMarker.

> One caveat is that if the user zooms in on the map while the animation is running, the marker will move from its path and then try to return. It might be a good idea to disable the map zoom until the animation has finished.

To animate your markers, perform the following steps:

1. Add a reference to the JavaScript file. No CSS file is required for this plugin:
   ```
   <script src="AnimatedMarker.js"></script>
   ```

2. Create a polyline to represent the path that the marker will be animated along:
   ```
   var line = L.polyline([[35.10306, -106.58695],[35.1046, -106.60137],[35.10727, -106.61734],[35.1046, -106.63794],[35.10601, -106.69287]]);
   ```

3. Create an `animatedMarker` variable. The marker takes an array of latitudes and longitudes. To get it, use the `getLatLngs()` method of the line you created:
   ```
   var animatedMarker = L.animatedMarker(line.getLatLngs());
   ```

4. Add the animated marker layer to the map. In this example, you will also add the line so that you can see it as a reference:
   ```
   map.addLayer(line);
   map.addLayer(animatedMarker);
   ```

When you open your map, it should look like the following screenshot:

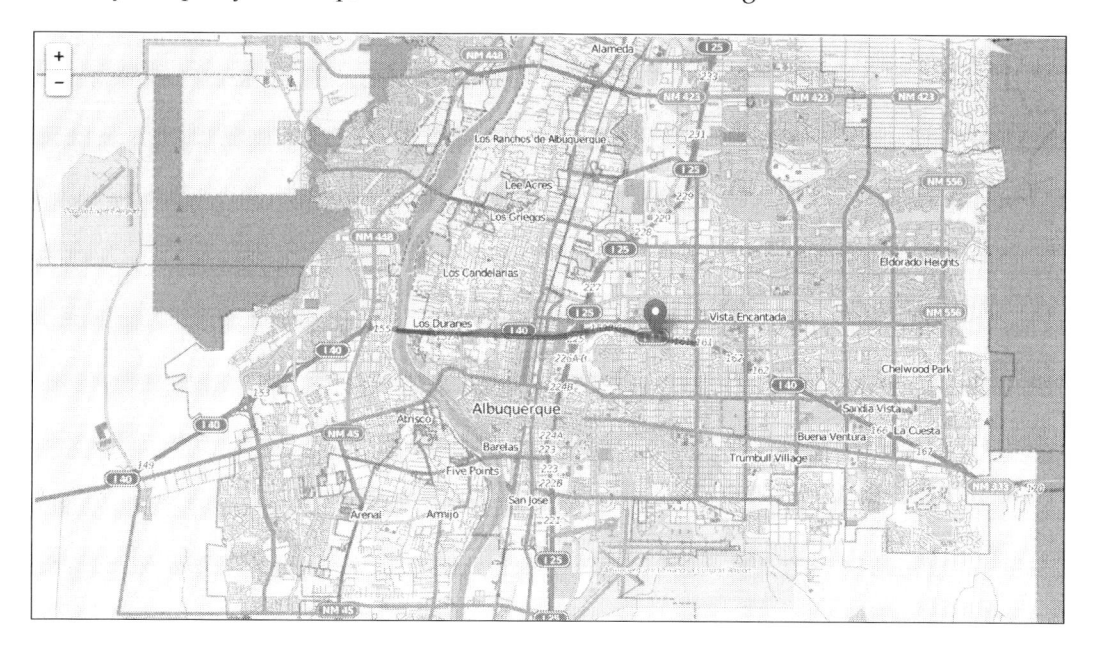

Creating Custom Markers

Because you did not pass any options to the marker, it will take a minute to start moving and will move fairly slowly across the blue line. The plugin has the following options:

- `distance`
- `interval`
- `autoStart`
- `onEnd`

The `distance` and `interval` options set the rate at which the marker will travel along the line. Distance is measured in meters, and interval is measured in milliseconds. Since it is a rate, an option of {distance:100, interval 1000} would be slower than an option of {distance:300, interval:1000}. In the first setting, the marker covers 100 meters in one second, and in the second setting, it would cover three times the distance in the same time.

The `autoStart` option is set to `true` by default. If you set it to `false`, you can call a `start()` method on the marker when you are ready. In the code used in the following steps, you will make a map with two buttons: **Start** and **Stop**. Using `autoStart:false`, you will allow the user to determine when to start the marker and when to stop it along its path:

1. Building on the previous example using the same line and marker, add an option to the marker for `distance` and `interval` and set `autoStart` to `false`:

   ```
   var line = L.polyline([[35.10306, -106.58695],[35.1046,
   -106.60137],[35.10727, -106.61734],[35.1046,
   -106.63794],[35.10601, -106.69287]]);
   var animatedMarker =
   L.animatedMarker(line.getLatLngs(),{autoStart: false,
   distance: 600, interval: 900});
   ```

2. Write a `start()` and `stop()` function to control the animation. Call the `start()` and `stop()` methods on the marker in the corresponding function:

   ```
   function start(){animatedMarker.start();}
   function stop(){animatedMarker.stop();}
   ```

3. In the HTML, before the `</body>` tag, add two buttons and set their `onClick` event equal to the corresponding function:

   ```
   <button onclick="start()">Start</button>
   <button onclick="stop()">Stop</button>
   ```

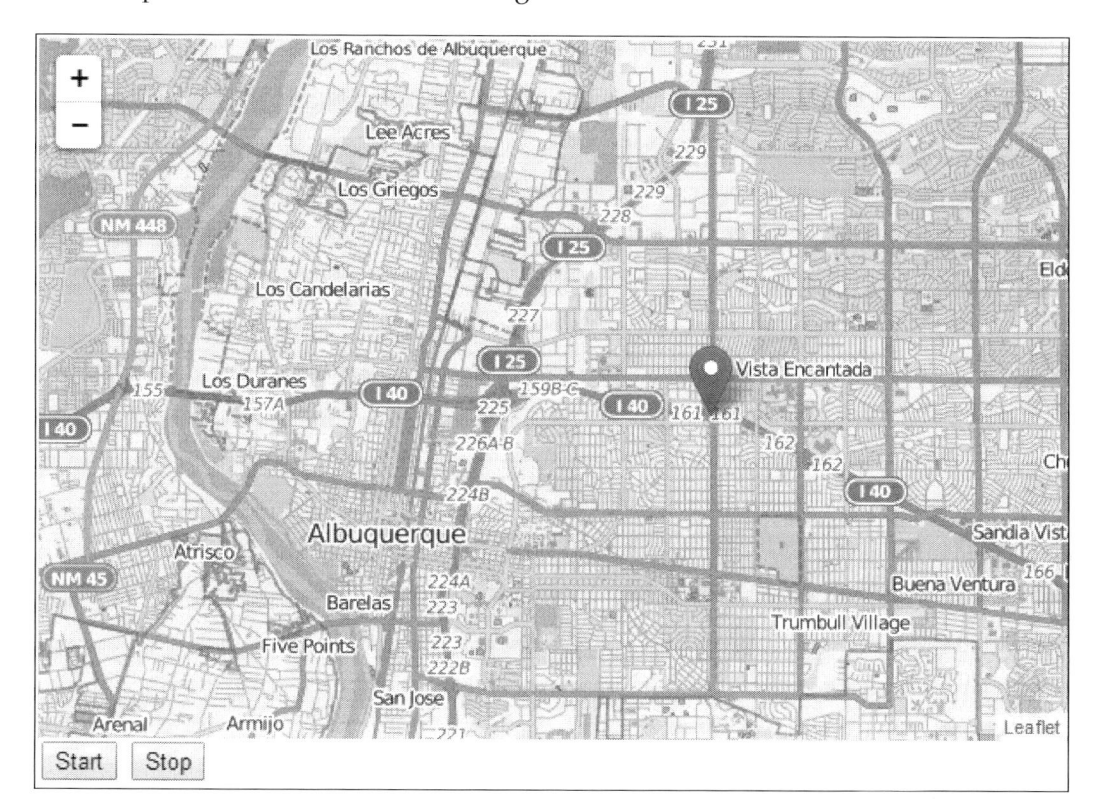

Your map should look like the following screenshot:

The marker will not move until the user clicks on the **Start** button. When the user clicks on the **Stop** button, the marker will not stop immediately. Animation occurs in segments along each segment of the polyline. When the marker reaches the endpoint of a segment, it will stop and not resume until the user clicks on **Start** again.

The last setting was `onEnd`. This option allows you to specify a callback function that will run when the marker gets to the end of the line. In the code in the following steps, you will use the bounce marker plugin you learned about earlier in this chapter to make the marker bounce and then disappear when it finishes. Follow the next set of steps to create your map:

1. Building on the previous example, add a reference to the bounce marker plugin:

   ```
   <script src="bouncemarker.js"></script>
   ```

2. Create the bounce marker at the last point of the line:

   ```
   b = new L.Marker([35.10601, -106.69287], {bounceOnAdd: true});
   ```

Creating Custom Markers

3. Edit the animated marker to include the `onEnd` option with an anonymous function. The anonymous function will add the bounce marker to the map, make it bounce, remove the animated marker, and then wait 900 milliseconds and call a `bye()` function, which will remove the bounce marker. The waiting will allow the marker to disappear after the bouncing is finished. This slows the process down so that the animation is not so abrupt. You could also use the callback function available to the bounce marker instead of the `bye()` function:

```
var animatedMarker = L.animatedMarker(line.
getLatLngs(),{autoStart: false, distance: 600, interval: 900,
onEnd: function() {b.addTo(map);b.bounce({duration: 100, height:
50});map.removeLayer(animatedMarker);setTimeout('bye()',900);}});5
0});map.removeLayer(animatedMarker);setTimeout('bye()',900);}});
```

Your map will look exactly the same as the previous example. When the marker reaches the end of the line, it will appear to bounce and disappear from the map. A fun project using custom and animated markers would be to recreate the Boston Marathon using a custom marker for each of the finishers and setting its rate to their actual race rate. When you click on the **Start** button, you could replay the race.

Using markers for data visualization

You have learned about several different marker types that still look like your typical marker. In this section, you will learn how to add markers that create a pie and bar chart—not exactly your standard marker.

Using the Leaflet Data Visualization Framework plugin

The Leaflet Data Visualization Framework plugin allows you to create markers that are just shapes: a standard pin style marker with a shape cutout, a star marker, and a polygon marker. It also allows you to add pie chart and bar chart markers to your map.

> The Leaflet Data Visualization Framework plugin also has markers for radial bar charts, coxcomb charts, stacked and radial meter markers, as well as a data layer, choropleth layer, and a legend control. This is a plugin worth exploring. You can download it at `http://humangeo.github.io/leaflet-dvf/`.

Creating basic markers

Creating basic markers is straightforward. The code used in the following steps will walk you through making a marker, a polygon marker, and a star marker:

1. First, create a reference to the CSS and two JavaScript files:

   ```
   <link rel="stylesheet" href="dvf.css" />
   <script src="Leaflet-dvf.js"></script>
   <script src="Leaflet-dvf.markers.js"></script>
   ```

2. Next, create the markers. What really makes this plugin stand out with regards to the standard markers is that you can use any of the options in the L.Path class. This allows you to fully customize your markers. Creating the markers requires you to select the marker type— MapMarker, RegularPolygonMarker, or StarMarker—and then select the options:

   ```
   var marker = new L.MapMarker([35.10418, -106.62987], {
       radius: 30,
   fillOpacity:0.5,
   fillColor:'orange',
   color:'purple',
   innerRadius:7,
   numberOfSides:4,
   rotation:10
       });
   map.addLayer(marker);

   var polygonmarker = new L.RegularPolygonMarker([35,-106], {
       numberOfSides: 3,
       rotation: 10,
       radius: 10,
   fillColor:'green',
   fillOpacity:1,
   opacity:1,
   weight:1,
   radius:30
   });
   map.addLayer(polygonmarker);
   var star = new L.StarMarker([35,-107], {numberOfPoints:8,
   opacity:1, weight:2, fillOpacity:0,radius:30});
   map.addLayer(star);
   ```

Creating Custom Markers

When you open your map, it will look like the following screenshot:

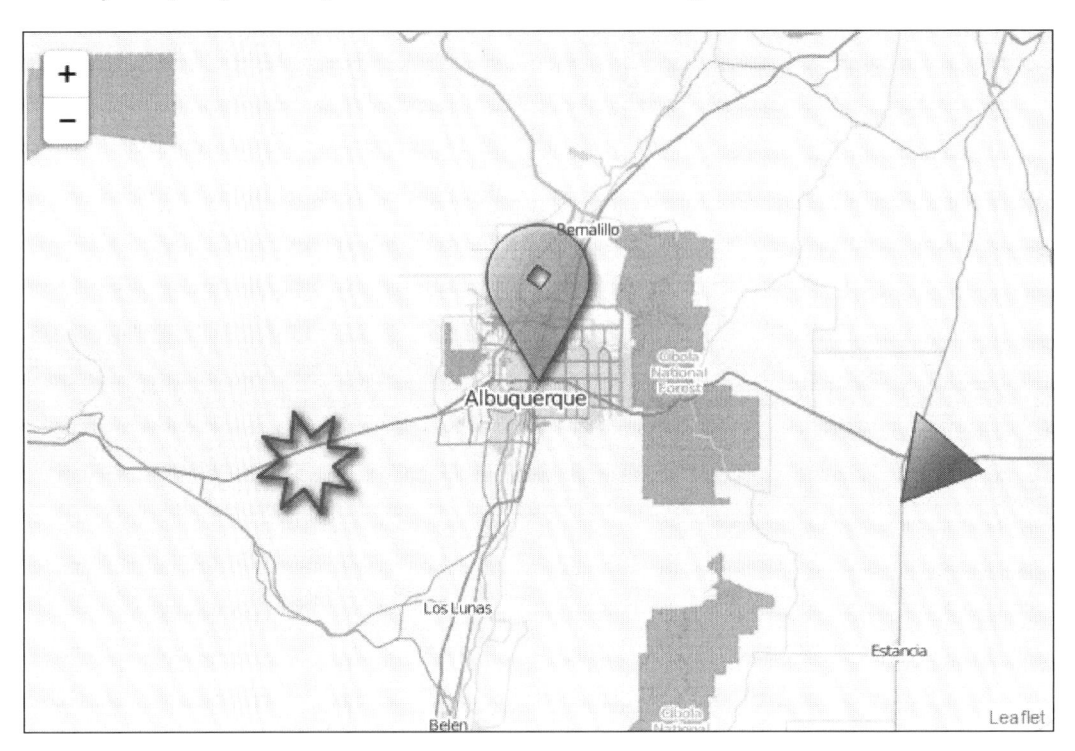

There are too many options to list here, but to see them, go to the documentation for the plugin at https://github.com/humangeo/Leaflet-dvf/wiki/6.-Markers and the documentation for the Leaflet `path` class at http://Leafletjs.com/reference.html#path. The plugin options you will use the most for each marker are explained in the following sections.

MapMarker options

The `MapMarker` options used are as follows:

- `numberOfSides`: The inner hole is determined by the number of sides: three for a triangle, four for a square. The larger the number, the closer to a circle it will be. If you leave this option blank, it will default to a circle.
- `rotation`: This helps you rotate the hole in the middle. This, of course, only works on shapes that are not a circle.
- `radius`: This is the size of the marker.
- `innerRadius`: This is the size of the hole in the middle.

[102]

RegularPolygonMarker options

The `RegularPolygonMarker` options used are as follows:

- `numberOfSides`: This is the shape of the marker.
- `rotation`: This is the orientation of the marker. If you create a four-sided polygon and leave this blank, it will be a square. If you add rotation, you can make the corners point in any direction.
- `radius`: This is the size of the marker.
- `innerRadius`: This is the size of the hole in the middle.

StarMarker options

The `StarMarker` options used are as follows:

- `numberOfPoints`: This defines how many points the start should have
- `rotation`: This is the orientation of the marker
- `radius`: This is the size of the marker
- `innerRadius`: This is the size of the hole in the middle

Bar and pie chart markers

Adding chart markers to your map allows you to show multiple pieces of data for a single point or polygon. For example, you could map all of the census blocks in your state and, using the center point of each block, you could place a chart showing the age distributions. This allows you to present a lot of data quickly and visually.

Making a bar or pie chart with the Leaflet Data Visualization Framework plugin only requires you to create an `options` object and pass it to the marker. The following steps will show you how to do both:

1. Create an `options` object with data and chart options. The data needs the name of the data category and the value. In the chart options object, you pass all of the options to style your chart. Three important options are `minValue`, `maxValue`, and `maxHeight`. These should, under most circumstances, be the same for all the categories. If you allow one category to have `maxHeight` higher than the rest, it can be displayed as a larger bar than another category with a higher value. Think of this as setting the *x* and *y* axis scales in Excel. All the data should be within the same scale of the lowest value to the highest value. Changing the `maxHeight` option will also make your chart larger or smaller. The options outside of the chart options are for the stroke or outline of the chart.

Creating Custom Markers

When creating a pie chart, the `radius` option allows you to adjust the size of the marker:

```
var options = {
    data: {
        'data1': 20,
        'data2': 50,
        'data3': 10,
        'data4': 20
    },
    chartOptions: {
        'data1': {
            fillColor: 'blue',
            minValue: 0,
            maxValue: 50,
            maxHeight: 30,
            },
        'data2': {
            fillColor: 'red',
            minValue: 0,
            maxValue: 50,
            maxHeight: 30,
            },
        'data3': {
            fillColor: 'green',
            minValue: 0,
            maxValue: 50,
            maxHeight: 30,
            },
        'data4': {
            fillColor: 'yellow',
            minValue: 0,
            maxValue: 50,
            maxHeight: 30,
            }
    },
    weight: 1,
    color: '#000000',
radius:30,
fillOpacity:1
};
```

2. Next, create the markers, pass the options, and add them to the map:

```
var bar = new L.BarChartMarker([35.10418, -106.62987],
options);
map.addLayer(bar);

var pie= new L.PieChartMarker([35,-107],options);
map.addLayer(pie);
```

Chapter 4

When you open your map, it should look like the following screenshot. When you hover over one of the data categories, you will see the color, category name, and value.

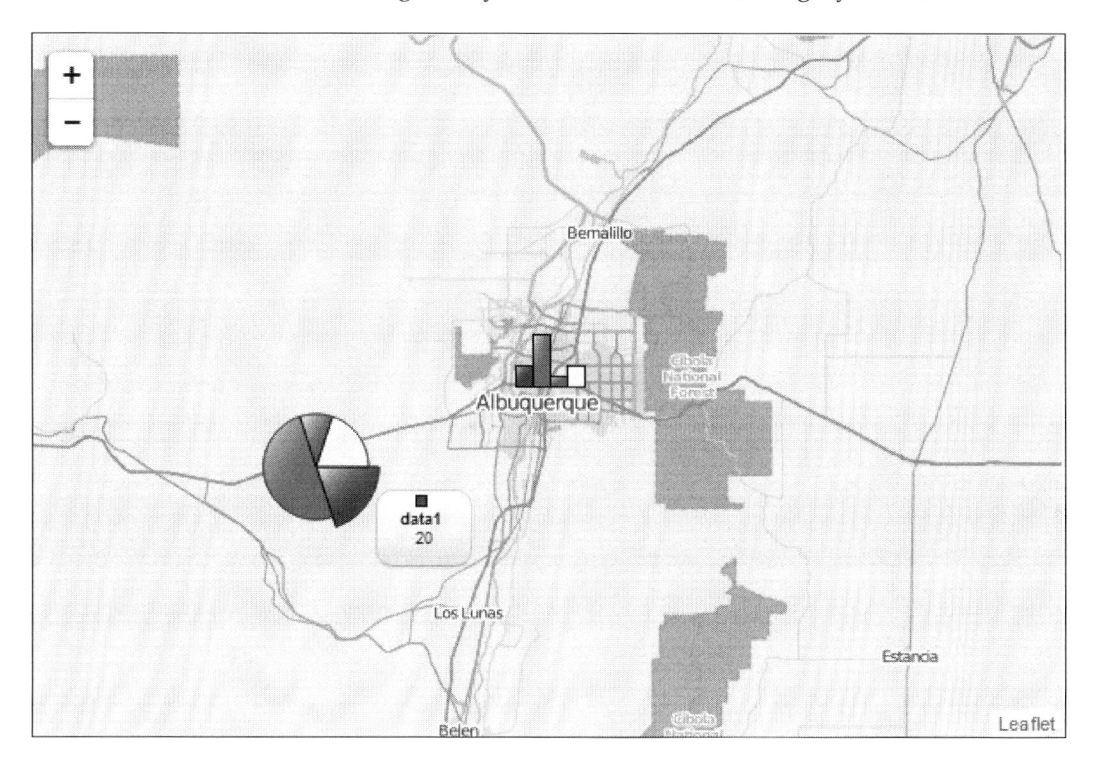

Summary

In this chapter, you learned how to add custom markers to your Leaflet map. You can now draw your own markers or use pre-existing images. You can also use plugins to load markers from Twitter, Font Awesome, and Mapbox. Lastly, you now know how to create bar chart and pie chart markers to visualize data in the form of a marker. At this point, you have acquired enough knowledge of Leaflet to build almost any style of map you can think of.

In the next chapter, you will learn how to use **Economic and Social Research Institute (ESRI)** data in your Leaflet map. As the most widely used GIS platform, you will most certainly run in to its data formats.

5
ESRI in Leaflet

As you start making more maps and looking for geospatial data to work with, you will almost certainly run into the file type shapefile (.shp). **Economic and Social Research Institute (ESRI)** is the creator of the most widely used GIS system, ArcGIS, and the shapefile is one of their data formats.

You may see another format called geodatabase with a .gdb extension. Even if you never run into a shapefile or geodatabase, you will eventually run into a REST service that is an endpoint to an ArcServer installation.

> ArcServer is an ESRI product for distributing GIS services and web mapping applications. It is separate from ArcGIS, which refers to the desktop application to create maps and geographic data.

The more data formats you know how to consume in your Leaflet maps, the less time you will need to spend converting data to suit your needs. In this chapter, you will learn how to consume ESRI formats and services in Leaflet.

In this chapter, we will cover the following topics:

- ESRI basemaps
- Working with shapefiles
- Displaying a dynamic map layer
- Heatmaps
- Geocoding and reverse geocoding
- Query layers

ESRI basemaps

ESRI provides eight different basemaps that you can use in your Leaflet map. The eight layers are the following:

- Streets
- Topographic
- National Geographic
- Oceans
- Gray
- Dark gray
- Imagery
- Shaded relief

In addition to the eight basemaps, there are six basemap label layers, `OceansLabels`, `GrayLabels`, `DarkGrayLabels`, `ImageryLabels`, `ImageryTransportation`, and `ShadedReliefLabels`, to compliment the basemaps. If that is not enough, there is also a retina version of each basemap.

To use an ESRI basemap, follow these steps:

1. First, add a reference to the ESRI-leaflet file. It is in beta, but that doesn't mean that it is not fully functional:

   ```
   <script src="http://cdn-geoweb.s3.amazonaws.com/esri-
      leaflet/0.0.1-beta.5/esri-Leaflet"></script>
   ```

   > On its GitHub repository, ESRI states that the library is on track to be moved from beta to production in 2014. You can find more information and download the additional files at https://github.com/Esri/esri-leaflet/.

2. Next, create an ESRI basemap layer, passing one of the eight options. In this example, use `Gray`. Always remember to add it to the map:

   ```
   var gray = L.esri.basemapLayer("Gray").addTo(map);
   ```

3. You now have a map with an ESRI basemap layer. The preceding code is the minimal code required to add a basemap. The ESRI basemap layer inherits from the Leaflet `L.TileLayer` class, and therefore, allows you to use all of the options, methods, and events available to any other Leaflet `L.TileLayer` class. One option that is extremely useful when building mobile maps is the `detectRetina` option. To use this option, just pass it after the basemap name as shown in the following code:

```
var gray = L.esri.basemapLayer("Gray",{detectRetina:
   true}).addTo(map);
```

Many examples that you find in the documentation will create the layers without assigning them to a variable, as shown in the following code from the ESRI website:

```
var map = L.map('map').setView([37.75,-122.45], 12);
L.esri.basemapLayer("Topographic").addTo(map);
```

When you do this, you have no way of calling methods or events on the layer unless you chain them. In the preceding example, you assigned the basemap to the variable `gray`, so you have access to all of the methods and events as shown in the following code:

```
gray.setOpacity(.75);
gray.on("load", alertme);
function alertme(){alert("ESRI Basemap Loaded");}
```

The preceding code modifies the opacity of the basemap layer and also subscribes to the `load` event. When the layer loads, it executes the `alertme()` function and pops up an alert stating that it is complete.

The last thing you may need to do with your ESRI basemap layer is to add the corresponding label layer. To do so, just add another basemap layer, passing the label layer as shown in the following code:

```
var grayLabel = L.esri.basemapLayer("GrayLabels").addTo(map);
```

Now, you will have a map that looks like this:

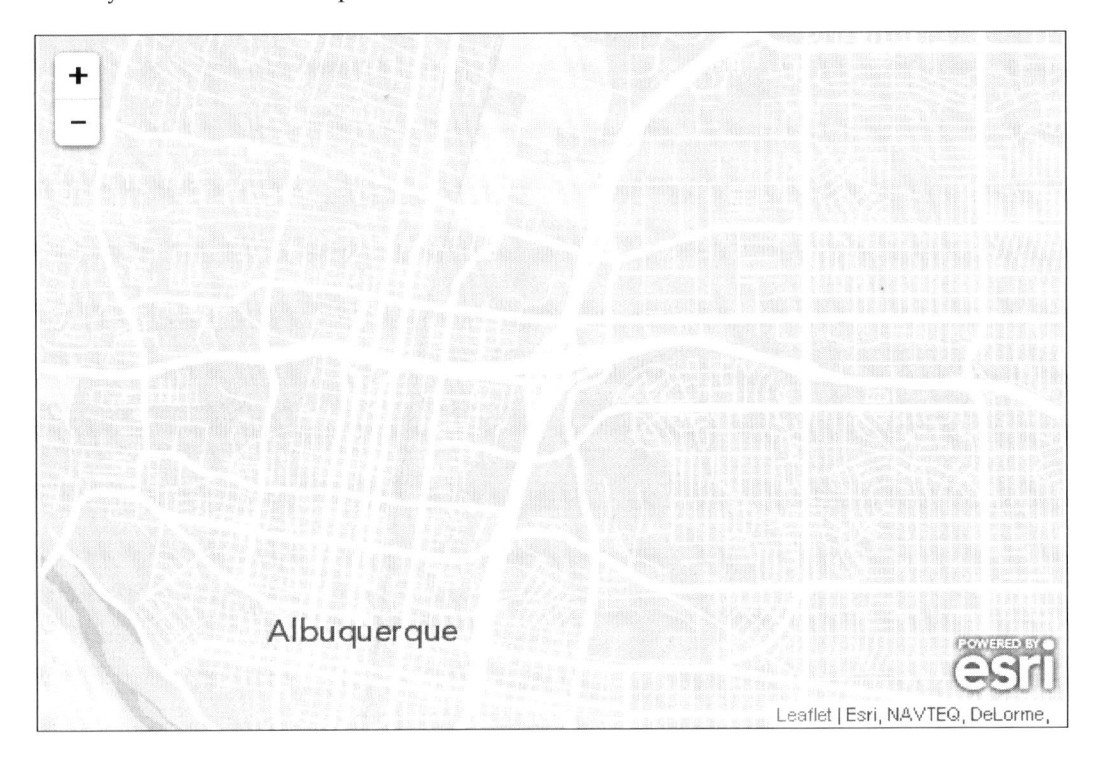

Using shapefiles in Leaflet

A shapefile is the most common geographic file type that you will most likely encounter. A shapefile is not a single file, but rather several files used to create geographic features on a map. When you download a shapefile, you will have `.shp`, `.shx`, and `.dbf` at a minimum. These files are the shapefiles that contain the geometry, the index, and a database of attributes. Your shapefile will most likely include a projection file (`.prj`) that will tell that application the projection of the data so the coordinates make sense to the application. In the examples, you will also have a `.shp.xml` file that contains metadata and two spatial index files, `.sbn` and `.sbx`.

To find shapefiles, you can usually search for open data and a city name. In this example, we will be using a shapefile from ABQ Data, the City of Albuquerque data portal. You can find more data on this at `http://www.cabq.gov/abq-data`. When you download a shapefile, it will most likely be in the ZIP format because it will contain multiple files.

To open a shapefile in Leaflet using the `leaflet-shpfile` plugin, follow these steps:

1. First, add references to two JavaScript files. The first, `leaflet-shpfile`, is the plugin, and the second depends on the shapefile parser, `shp.js`:

   ```
   <script src="leaflet.shpfile.js"></script>
   <script src="shp.js"></script>
   ```

2. Next, create a new shapefile layer and add it to the map. Pass the layer path to the zipped shapefile:

   ```
   var shpfile = new L.Shapefile('council.zip');
   shpfile.addTo(map);
   ```

Your map should display the shapefile as shown in the following screenshot:

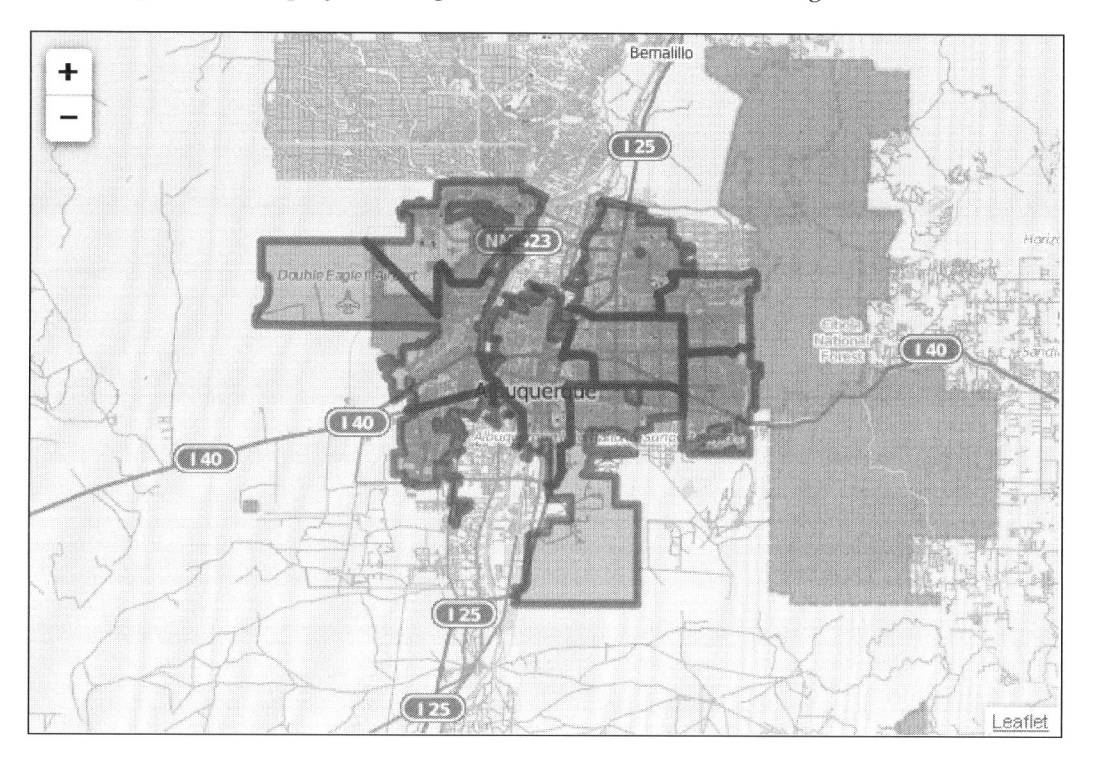

ESRI in Leaflet

Performing the preceding steps will add the shapefile to the map. You will not be able to see any individual feature properties. When you create a shapefile layer, you specify the data, followed by specifying the options. The options are passed to the `L.geoJson` class. To add a pop up or to style the features, you use the same process that you learned in *Chapter 2, Mapping GeoJSON Data*. The following code shows you how to add a pop up to your shapefile layer:

```
var shpfile = new
    L.Shapefile('council.zip',{onEachFeature:function(feature,
    layer) {
layer.bindPopup("<a
href='"+feature.properties.WEBPAGE+"'>Page</a><br><a href='"+feature.
properties.PICTURE+"'>Image</a>");
}});
```

In the preceding code, you pass `council.zip` to the shapefile, and for options, you use the `onEachFeature` option, which takes a function. In this case, you use an anonymous function and bind the pop up to the layer. In the text of the pop up, you concatenate your HTML with the name of the property you want to display using the format `feature.properties.NAME-OF-PROPERTY`. To find the names of the properties in a shapefile, you can open `.dbf` and look at the column headers. However, this can be cumbersome, and you may want to add all of the shapefiles in a directory without knowing its contents. If you do not know the names of the properties for a given shapefile, the following example shows you how to get them and then display them with their value in a pop up:

```
var holder=[];

for (var key in feature.properties){
holder.push(key+": "+feature.properties[key]+"<br>");
popupContent=holder.join("");
layer.bindPopup(popupContent);
}
shapefile.addTo(map);
```

In the preceding code, you first create an array to hold all of the lines in your pop up, one for each key/value pair. Next, you run a `for` loop that iterates through the object, grabbing each key and concatenating the key name with the value and a line break. You push each line into the array and then join all of the elements into a single string. When you use the `.join()` method, it will separate each element of the array in the new string with a comma.

You can pass empty quotes to remove the comma. Lastly, you bind the pop up with the string as the content and then add the shapefile to the map.

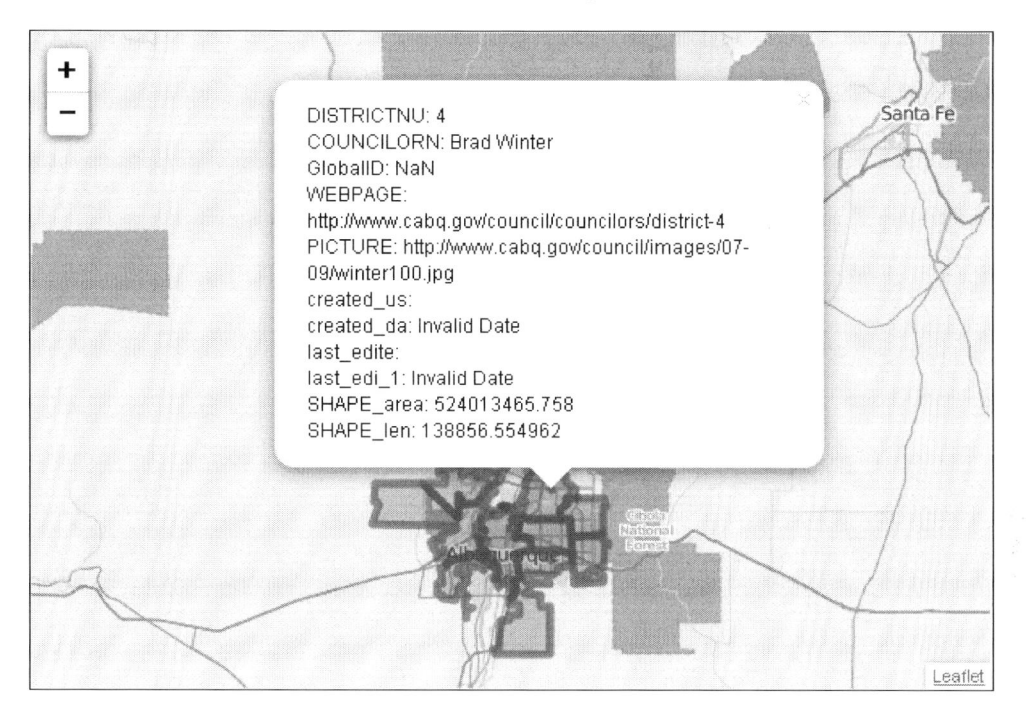

You now have a map that looks like the following screenshot:

The shapefile also takes a style option. You can pass any of the path class options, such as the color, opacity, or stroke, to change the appearance of the layer. The following code creates a red polygon with a black outline and sets it slightly transparent:

```
var shpfile = new
L.Shapefile('council.zip',{style:function(feature){return
   {color:"black",fillColor:"red",fillOpacity:.75}}});
```

Consuming ESRI services

In the first example of this chapter, you learned how to use the `esri-leaflet` plugin for basemaps. You then learned how to use a plugin to work with the most common ESRI file format: the shapefile. While you will most certainly run into a shapefile, you will increasingly find yourself running into ESRI services that provide endpoints that you can connect to and consume geographic services from. With the `esri-leaflet` plugin, you can connect to these services, and besides basemaps, display five other layer types:

- The tiled map layer
- The dynamic map layer

ESRI in Leaflet

- The feature layer
- The clustered feature layer
- The heatmap feature layer

Once you know how to add one of these layers, you can add any of the others because the process is almost identical. The only differences are the available options and methods, which are well documented in the API at http://esri.github.io/esri-leaflet/api-reference/. Later in this chapter, we will learn how to create a heatmap feature layer, but for now, let's see how to add a dynamic map layer.

On the City of Albuquerque data page at http://www.cabq.gov/abq-data, select the public art dataset. You will be presented with the contents of the directory. You can read the MetaData.pdf file to learn about the data source, download a Google Earth .KMZ file, download or link to a JSON file, or consume a PublicArtREST service.

> The JSON file available from the City of Albuquerque data page is ESRI JSON. It is not GeoJSON, and thus, it will not be compatible without some conversion.

Click on the link for PublicArtREST and you will be presented with the details of this service. Scrolling to the bottom of the page will tell you the available fields. This will be very useful when designing the pop ups. Now that you know where to find the service, follow these steps to add it to your map:

1. First, add a reference to the ESRI-leaflet file:

   ```
   <script src="http://cdn-geoweb.s3.amazonaws.com/esri-
     leaflet/0.0.1-beta.5/esri-Leaflet"></script>
   ```

2. Create a dynamic map layer by copying the link to the REST service—all dynamic map layers will end in /mapserver. We removed /0 from the URL, which means that we are now loading the entire map file. In the following code, set the opacity option to 0.75 and add the layer to the map:

   ```
   var art = L.esri.dynamicMapLayer("http://coagisweb.cabq.gov/
   arcgis/re
      st/services/public/PublicArt/MapServer).addTo(map);
   ```

3. Lastly, bind a pop up using a function that will return the content. In the following code, use the format feature.features[0].properties.NAME-OF-PROPERTY:

   ```
   art.bindPopup(function (err, feature) {
   return feature.features[0].properties.TITLE+"<br> by:
     <b>"+feature.features[0].properties.ARTIST;   });
   ```

[114]

Your map will now look like this:

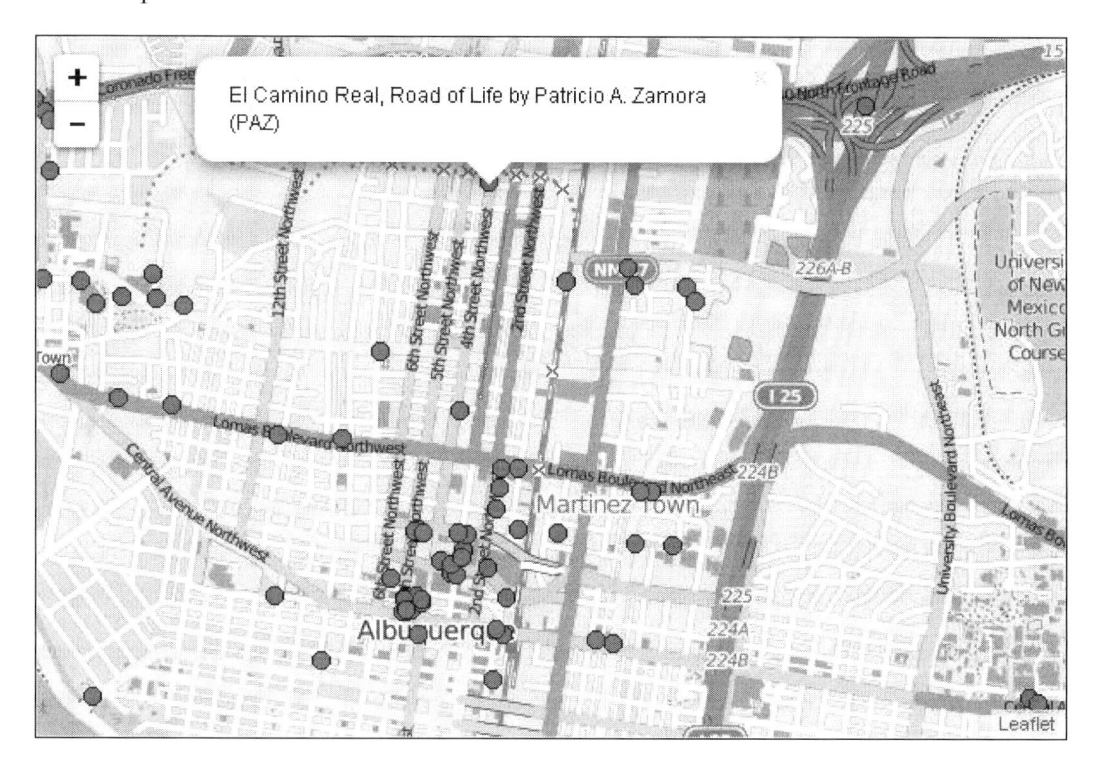

Heatmaps with ESRI in Leaflet

In *Chapter 3, Creating Heatmaps and Choropleth Maps*, you learned about several plugins that you can use to create heatmaps. The `esri-leaflet` plugin also has a heatmap layer that will allow you to pass an ESRI service as the data. To create a heatmap using the `esri-leaflet` plugin, follow these steps:

1. First, add a reference to the ESRI-leaflet file, and since the heatmap layer is not included in the core build of the `esri-leaflet` plugin, you will need to reference an additional ESRI file, `esri-leaflet-heatmap-feature-layer.js`. The ESRI heatmap layer requires `leaflet-heat.js`, so you need to add a reference to that as well:

   ```
   <script src="http://cdn-geoweb.s3.amazonaws.com/esri-
      leaflet/0.0.1-beta.5/esri-Leaflet"></script>
   <script src="esri-leaflet-heatmap-feature-
      layer.js"></script>
   <script src="leaflet-heat.js"></script>
   ```

2. Create your map and basemap as you normally would and then add the heatmap layer. The heatmap layer requires a link to a feature layer service and acquires all of the options available in `leaflet-heat.js`. Add the layer to the map:

```
url= ("http://services.arcgis.com/pmcEyn9tLWCoX7Dm/arcgis/rest/
    services/USGS_Earthquakes_Excel_Layer/FeatureServer/0";
var heatmap = new L.esri.HeatmapFeatureLayer(url, {
            radius: 50,
    blur:90,
    maxZoom:10
}).addTo(map);
```

> To see a list of the available services from ESRI, browse to http://services.arcgis.com/rOo16HdIMeOBI4Mb/ArcGIS/rest/services/. The location of ArcServer services defaults to http://Server Name/ ArcGIS/rest/services.

Your map will look like the following screenshot:

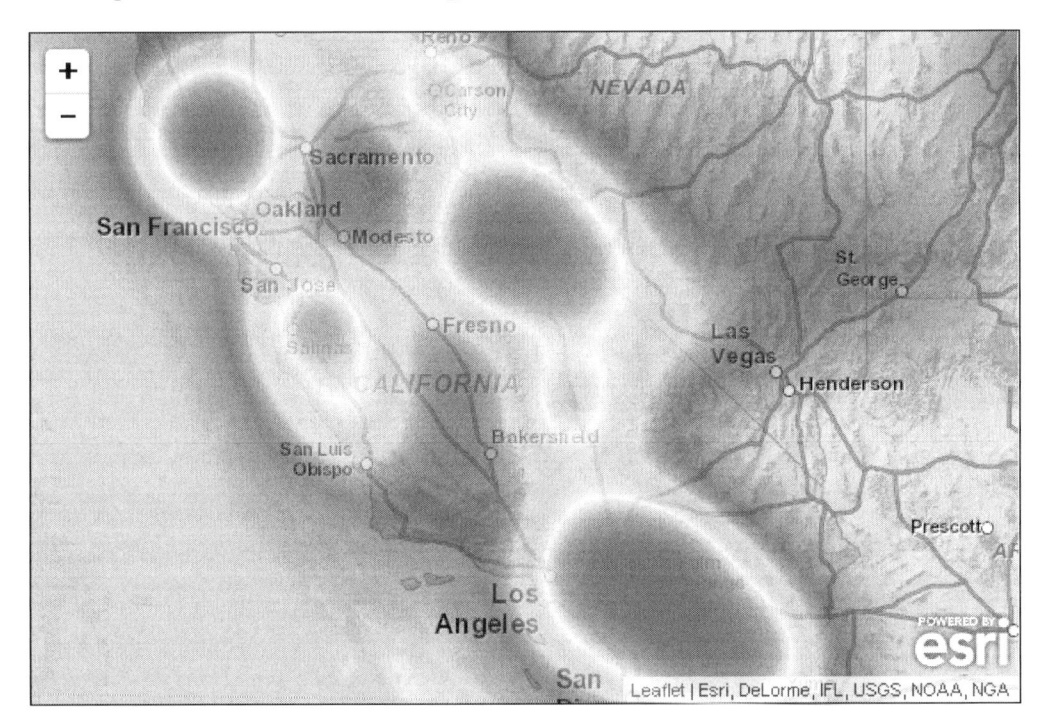

Geocoding addresses in Leaflet

Geocoding is the process by which you can enter an address and be taken to a point on the map. Geocoding functionality is not part of the Esri-leaflet core but is a separate plugin. You can find more information on the esri-leaflet-geocoder GitHub page at `https://github.com/Esri/esri-leaflet-geocoder`.

Geocoding – from an address to a point

The geocoding plugin places a search box below the zoom control. As you type an address, the search autocompletes and presents the possible options. You can either type the whole address or select from the list when the one you want is available. Clicking on an option or pressing enter will put a marker on the map at the location and zoom into it. To create a map with geocoding functionality, follow these steps:

1. Reference the CSS and JS files:

    ```
    <script src="http://cdn-geoweb.s3.amazonaws.com/esri-
       leaflet-geocoder/0.0.1-beta.3/esri-leaflet-geocoder.js"></
    script>
    <link rel="stylesheet" type="text/css" href="http://cdn-
       geoweb.s3.amazonaws.com/esri-leaflet-geocoder/0.0.1-
         beta.3/esri-leaflet-geocoder.css">
    ```

2. Create the control:

    ```
    var searchControl = new
       L.esri.Controls.Geosearch().addTo(map);
    ```

3. Create a layer where the result will be placed:

    ```
    var results = new L.LayerGroup().addTo(map);
    ```

4. Subscribe to the results event and add the marker:

    ```
    searchControl.on("results", function(data){
    results.clearLayers();
    results.addLayer(L.marker(data.results[0].latlng));
    ```

ESRI in Leaflet

Your map will now have a small magnifying glass under the zoom control, as shown in the following screenshot:

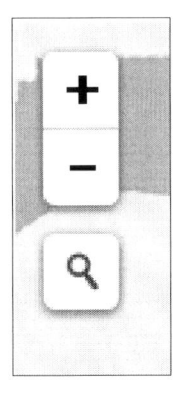

When you click on the magnifying glass, it will expand into a textbox. As you type, the textbox will autocomplete and guess the location that you are typing. Once you see the address you want, select it from the list. Your map should look like the following screenshot:

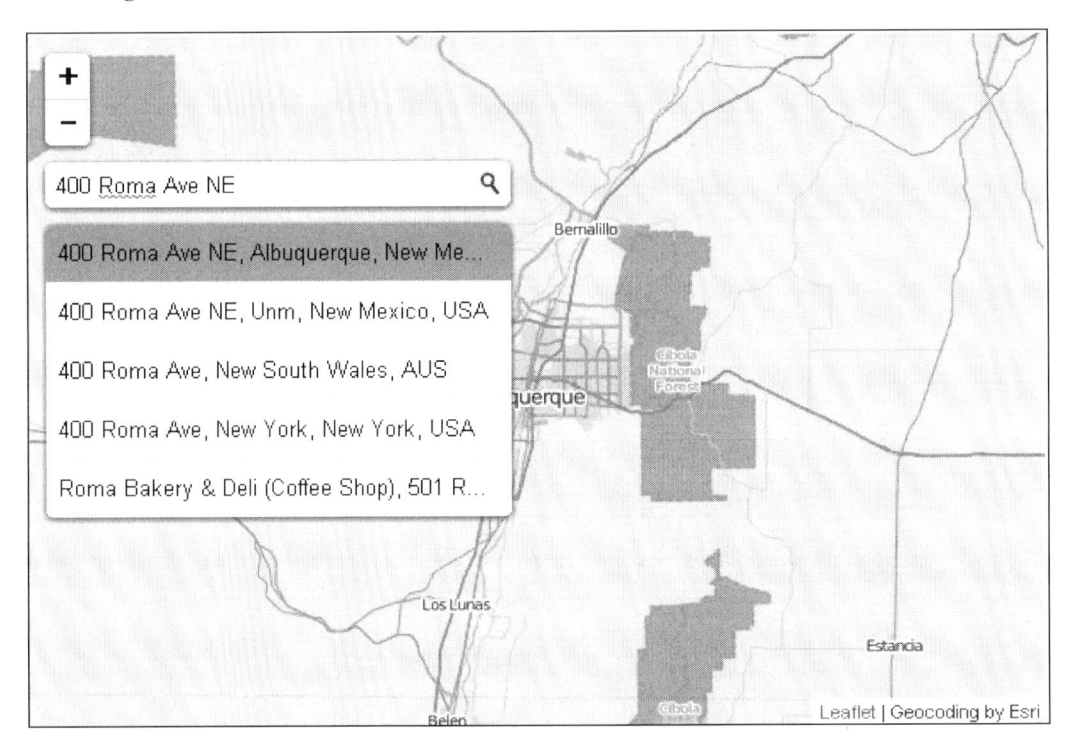

[118]

Once you have clicked on your selection, the map will automatically place a marker at the location and zoom into it. You will now have a map that looks like the following:

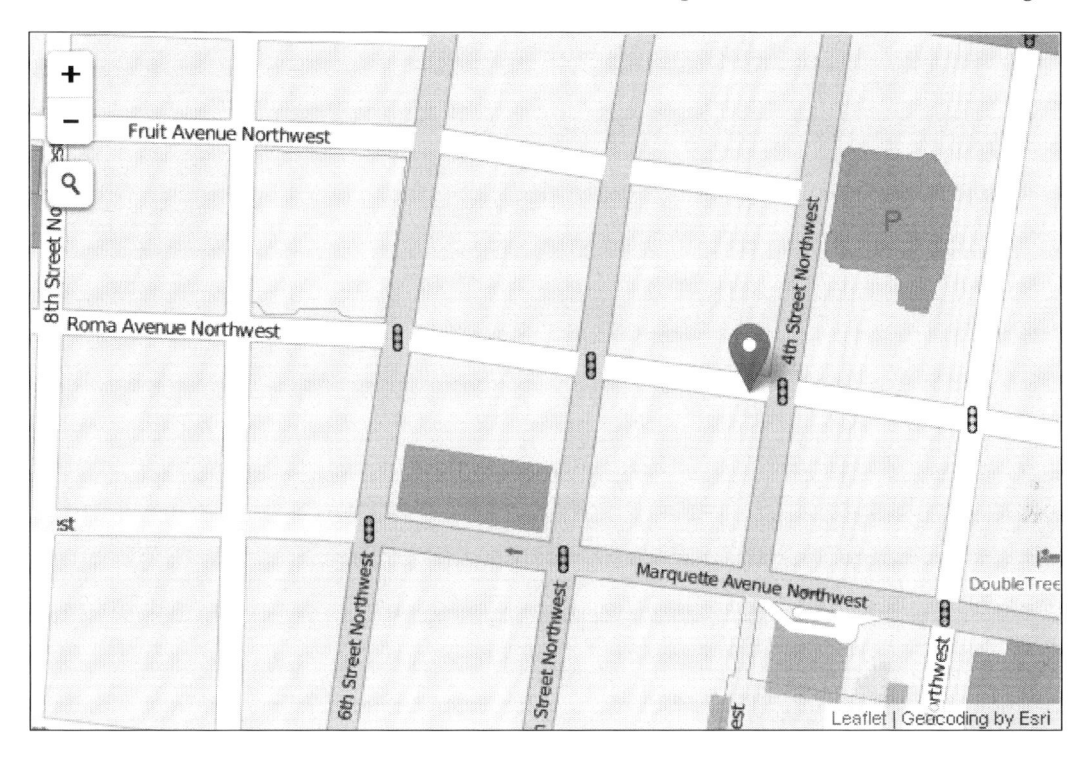

For the next example, you will use a URL to map an address.

Geocoding from URL parameters

In the last example, a user is able to load the map and enter an address to find it. In this example, you will allow the user to enter the address in the URL and be presented with a map that has zoomed into a marker at the location. To create the map, follow these steps:

1. First, add a reference to the `esri-leaflet-geocoder.js` file. You do not need the CSS file, as you did in the previous example, because you are not adding the search box:

   ```
   <script src="http://cdn-geoweb.s3.amazonaws.com/esri-
     leaflet-geocoder/0.0.1-beta.5/esri-leaflet-
       geocoder.js"></script>
   ```

2. Next, you need to get the parameter from the URL. In this example, a is chosen as the variable that will contain the address. To get the URL parameters, use location.search. This grabs everything after the question mark. You only want the address, so split it on the equals sign and then grab the second element of the returned array, y[1]. This will return %20 wherever there is a space in the URL, so use decodeURIComponent(y[1]) to remove them:

```
var x = location.search;
var y = x.split("=");
var temp=y[1];
var address = decodeURIComponent(temp);
var geocodeService = new L.esri.Services.Geocoding();
```

3. Create the geocoding service, passing the address, parameters, and a callback function. The function will create a marker from the first result and then set the view zoomed in on the marker:

```
geocodeService.geocode(address, {}, function(error,
  result){
L.marker(result[0].latlng).addTo(map);
map.setView(result[0].latlng,8);
});
```

Load the page and add ?a=400 roma ave ne,albuquerque,nm,usa after the URLgeocode.html file. Your map will load and look like this:

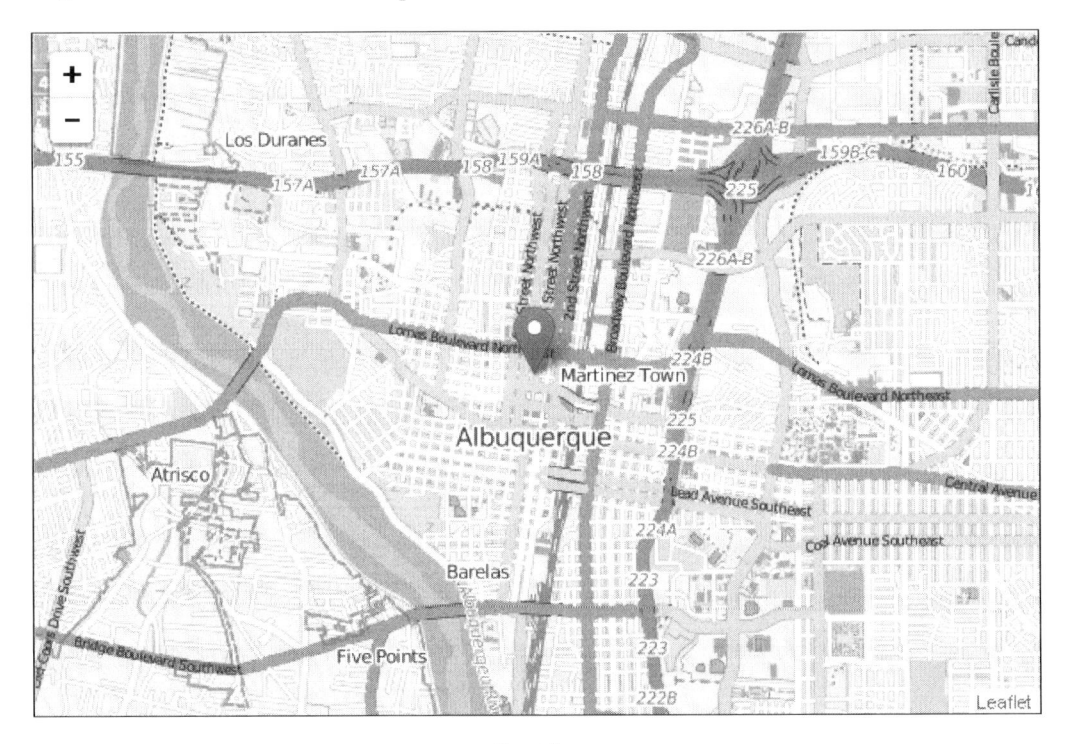

Reverse geocoding – using points to find addresses

Reverse geocoding does the exact opposite of geocoding. It takes a point on a map and finds its address. In this example, you will allow the user to click on the map and add a marker that has the address as a pop up. To create the map, follow these steps:

1. First, add a reference to the Esri-leaflet and `esri-leaflet-geocoder.js` files:

    ```
    <script src="http://cdn-geoweb.s3.amazonaws.com/esri-
      leaflet/0.0.1-beta.5/esri-Leaflet"></script>
    <script src="http://cdn-geoweb.s3.amazonaws.com/esri-
      leaflet-geocoder/0.0.1-beta.5/esri-leaflet-geocoder.js"></
    script>
    ```

2. Create a new geocoding service:

    ```
    var geocodeService = new L.esri.Services.Geocoding();
    ```

3. Subscribe to the `click` event and add a function that calls `reverse()`, passing longitude and latitude options, and a callback function. The callback function will create a marker, add it to the map, and then bind a pop up. The address is stored in the result object as `result.address`. This code will add a point every time you click on the map. To only have one point displayed, add `map.removeLayer(r)` before creating the marker:

    ```
    map.on('click', function(e){
    geocodeService.reverse(e.latlng, {}, function(error,
      result){
    r = L.marker(result.latlng).addTo(map).bindPopup(result.address
      ).openPopup();
        });
      });
    ```

ESRI in Leaflet

When you are finished, your map will look like this:

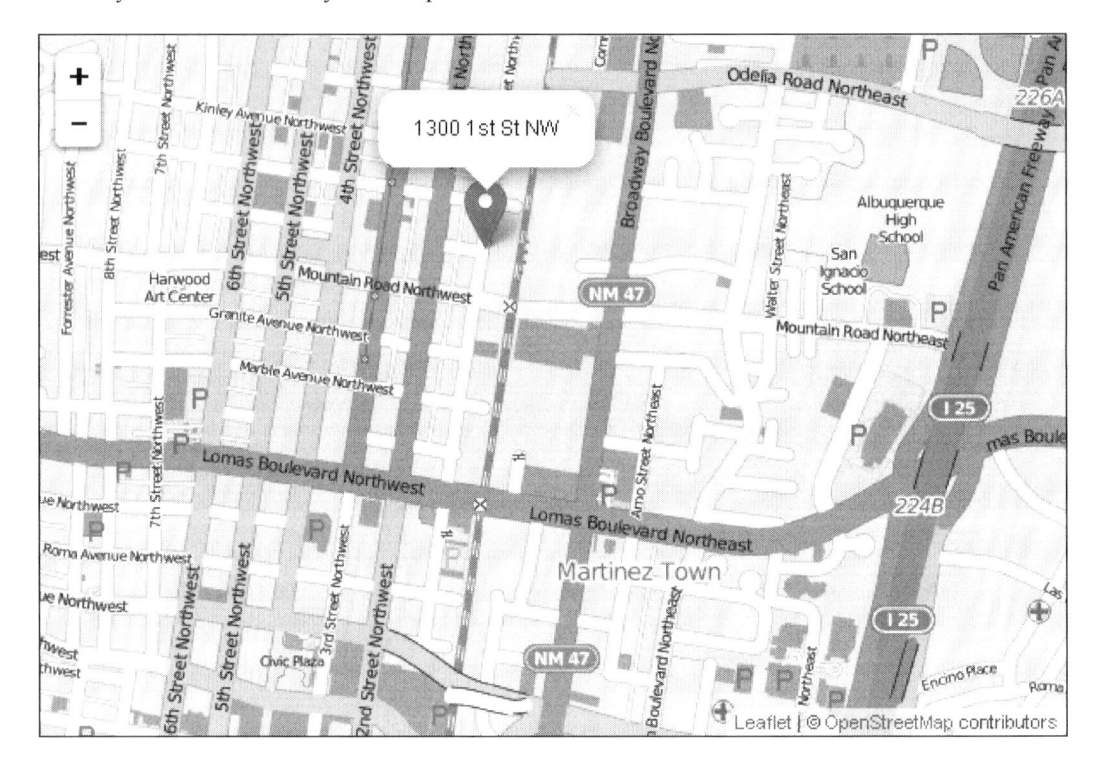

Query by attribute

When consuming a service, you usually load the entire layer. Sometimes, you may only want a subset of the layer data. Using a query will allow you to load only that subset that you are interested in. In this example, you will query a graffiti layer for open and closed cases. To create the map, follow these steps:

1. Reference the Esri-leaflet file as you have seen in the previous examples. You do not need any additional files. Style the `<div>` query using CSS:

    ```
    <style>
      #query {
        position: absolute;
        top: 10px;
        right: 10px;
        z-index: 10;
        background: white;
        padding: 1em;
      }
    ```

```
    #query select {
      font-size: 16px;
    }
</style>
```

2. Create the selection element and add `Open` and `Closed` as options:

```
<label>
 Status
  <select id="caseStatus">
    <option value=''>Clear Screen</option>
    <option value='Open'>Open</option>
    <option value='Closed'>Closed</option>
      </select>
</label>
```

3. Add a feature layer that connects to the graffiti service. Use the `pointToLayer` option to create a marker for each feature and add them to the map:

```
var graffiti =
  L.esri.featureLayer('http://services.arcgis.com/
  rOo16HdIMeOBI4Mb/ArcGIS/rest/services/Graffiti_Locations3
  /FeatureServer/0', {
  pointToLayer: function (geojson, latlng, feature) {
    return L.marker(latlng);
  },
}).addTo(map);
```

4. Create a `popupTemplate` variable. You can find the parameters in the layer by browsing to the link in the feature layer. Bind the pop up by creating a function that returns the template. The template allows you to pass the fields contained in the ESRI layer to the template. The field name goes in curly braces. Then, you can use the template as your string in `bindPopup()`:

```
var popupTemplate =
   "<h3>Details:</h3>Address:{Incident_Address_Display}<br>
Borough: {Borough}<br>Community Board:
{Community_Board}<br>Police Precinct:
  {Police_Precinct}<br>City_Council_District:
    {City_Council_District}<br>Created_Date:
  {Created_Date}<br>Status: {Status}<br>Resolution_Action:
  {Resolution_Action}<br>Closed_Date: {Closed_Date}<br>City:
{City}<br>State: {State}";
graffiti.bindPopup(function(feature){
return L.Util.template(popupTemplate, feature.properties)
      });
```

ESRI in Leaflet

5. Create an event for when the selection element changes. Pass the value of the current selection to the method `setWhere()`. This method refreshes the feature layer based on the `where` query. In this example, `where` is the value of the `status` property:

   ```
   caseStatus.addEventListener('change', function(){
   graffiti.setWhere('Status="'+caseStatus.value+'"');
   });
   ```

When you are finished, you can select **Closed**, and the map will look like this:

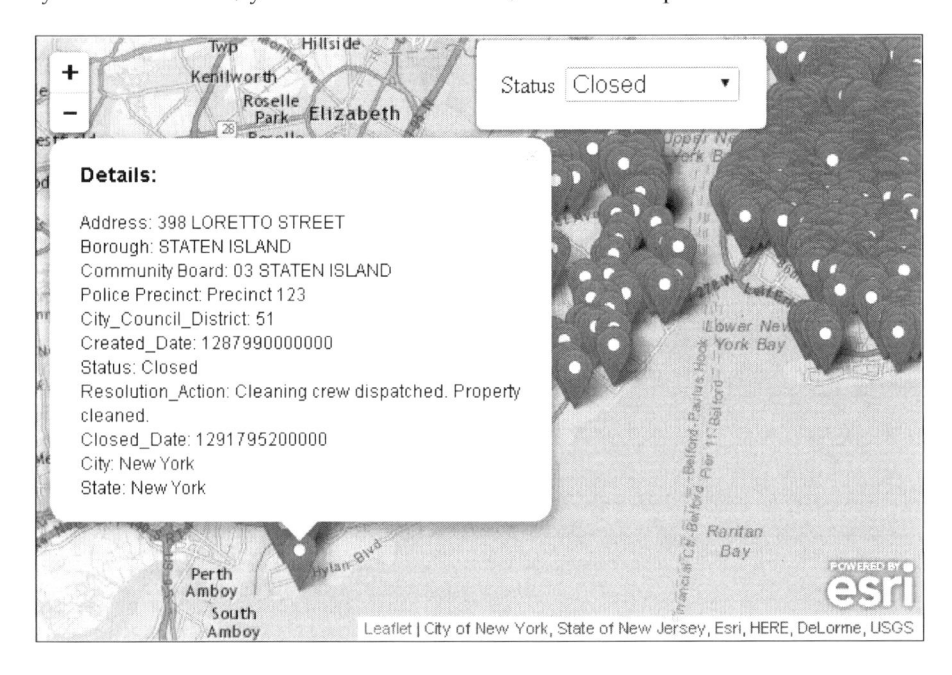

Query by proximity

In the previous example, you queried a feature layer based on an attribute. You can also query your feature layer based on its proximity to a point. In this example, you will query the layer based on the location of a mouse click. The following instructions will walk you through creating a proximity query:

1. Reference the Esri-leaflet file as you have in previous examples. Add the feature layer to the map. You will pass the `pointToLayer` option, returning `circleMarker` for each feature. You need to create the circle marker so that you can change the color of the marker in a later step:

   ```
   var graffiti = L.esri.featureLayer('http://services.arcgis.com/
     rOo16HdIMeOBI4Mb/ArcGIS/rest/services/
       Graffiti_Locations3/FeatureServer/0', {
   ```

```
      pointToLayer: function (geojson, latlng) {
         return L.circleMarker(latlng);
      },

   }).addTo(map);
```

2. Create a pop-up template using the feature properties. Bind the pop up to the feature as follows:

   ```
   var popupTemplate = "<h3>Details:</h3>Address:
      Incident_Address_Display}<br>Borough:
      {Borough}<br>Community Board: Community_Board}<br>Police
      Precinct: {Police_Precinct}<br>City_Council_District:
      City_Council_District}<br>Created_Date:
      {Created_Date}<br>Status: Status}<br>Resolution_Action:
      {Resolution_Action}<br>Closed_Date: Closed_Date}<br>City:
      {City}<br>State: {State}";
   graffiti.bindPopup(function(feature){
   return L.Util.template(popupTemplate, feature.properties)
      });
   ```

3. Create a query. If you browse to the service—place the URL of the query in your browser—and scroll to the bottom of the page, you will see on the last line that this service supports querying. Pass the query to the layer you want to query:

   ```
   var query =
   L.esri.Tasks.query('http://services.arcgis.com/
      rOo16HdIMeOBI4Mb/ArcGIS/rest/services/
      Graffiti_Locations3/FeatureServer
   /0');
   ```

4. Create an event for a mouse click and subscribe using the `runQuery()` function:

   ```
   map.on('click', runQuery);
   ```

5. Create a function, `runQuery()`, to be executed when the user clicks on the map. This function will do three things: it will execute a query using the `nearby()` method, passing the latitude and longitude of the mouse click and a distance of 804 meters (half mile); it will set the style of all of the circle markers to blue; and it will take the results of the query and pass the ID of every marker that is returned to a `style` function, turning them green. We used the circle marker in the second step so that we could change the color to highlight the query results:

   ```
   function runQuery(e){
   graffiti.query().nearby(e.latlng,804).ids(function
      (error,ids){
   graffiti.setStyle(function(){return { color: "blue"};});
   ```

```
   for(var i=0;i<ids.length;i++){graffiti.setFeatureStyle(ids[i],
     {color:"green"});}});
}
```

When you click on the map, it should look like this:

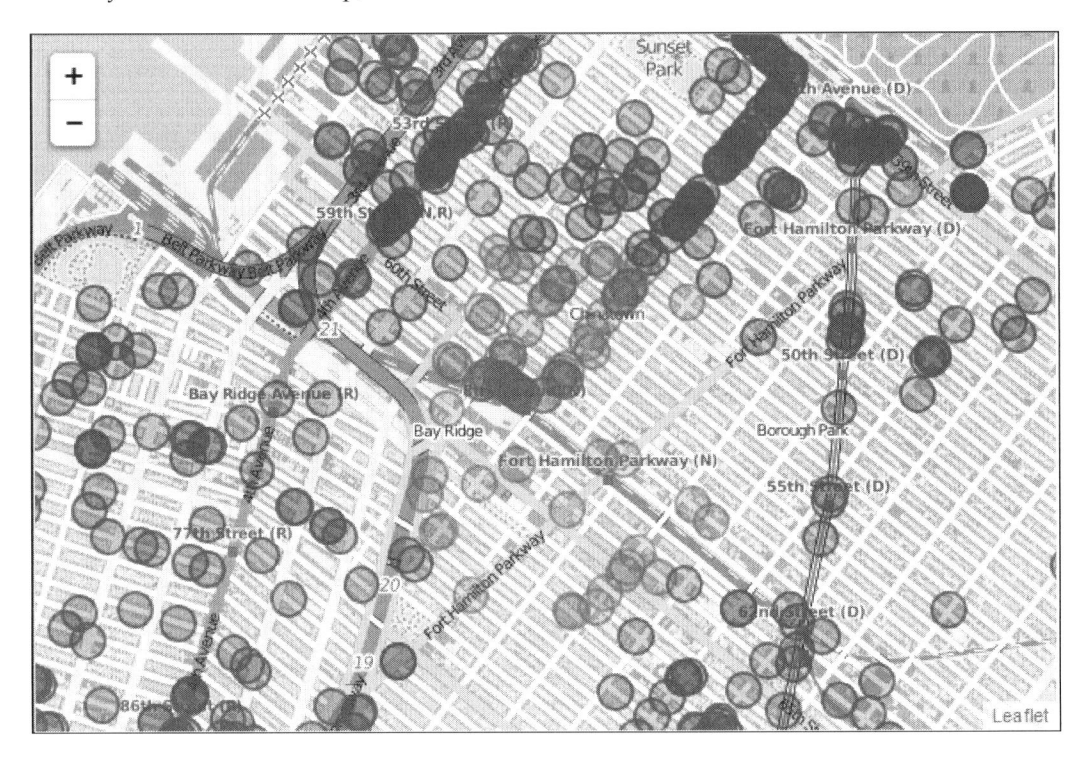

The green markers are all within half a mile of the user's click.

Summary

In this chapter, you learned how to use the most common file format for geographical data: the shapefile. You also learned how to use the `esri-leaflet` plugin to connect to ESRI services and add basemaps as well as five other ESRI layer types. You already learned about heatmaps previously, but in this chapter, you also learned how to consume ESRI services and add them as a heatmap. You learned how to geocode an address to a map and also how to reverse geocode a point to a street address. Lastly, you learned how to query an ESRI service first by attribute and then by location.

In the next chapter, you will combine everything you have learned to create an application using Leaflet with other programming languages.

6
Leaflet in Node.js, Python, and C#

In the first five chapters, you covered the fundamentals of Leaflet.js. You now know how to add a wide variety of basemaps from multiple sources and in several different formats. You can draw simple geometries as well as display data from servers, GeoJSON, and ESRI file formats. Creating visualizations from your data was covered in *Chapter 3*, *Creating Heatmaps and Choropleth Maps*. You also know how to customize the look and feel of your markers now and how to utilize plugins in order to add extra functionalities to your map.

In this last chapter, you will learn how to build applications utilizing Leaflet.js in three popular programming frameworks: Node.js, Python, and C#. In Node.js and Python, you will build a server to render your web page and allow for AJAX calls to display additional data. In the last example, using C#, you will build a desktop Windows application that embeds a web page into a form, connects to MongoDB, and retrieves data using a general search and a spatial search.

While you are not expected to have a working knowledge of either of these three frameworks, Node.js is a JavaScript framework and the examples should be easy to follow. The Python and C# examples might be a little different from what you are used to; however, the main ideas should be easy to grasp and they will give you an idea of how you can think of using Leaflet in larger applications. Furthermore, starting to think about how Leaflet can interact with the server side will expand your ability to dream up new and exciting applications, utilizing libraries and resources from multiple frameworks.

The first example will start with the most familiar framework, Node.js.

Building Leaflet applications with Node.js

Node.js is a JavaScript-based platform that builds non-blocking applications. The non-blocking feature is what has made Node.js extremely popular. Think about how you code. You complete tasks step-by-step. You might jump around in your code, calling functions and responding to events, but you wait until one action is complete before you start the next. With Node.js, you assign callbacks and move on to the next task or handle the next request. Take a database search, for example. In the following pseudocode, you retrieve a record and do something with it in the traditional manner:

```
var result = SELECT * from MyTable;
document.getElementById['results'].innerHTML= result;
```

In the example, you wait for the database to send back the results, and then you move on to displaying them. In Node.js, you would do something similar but assign a callback function, as shown in the following example:

```
function showResults(){document.getElementById['results'].innerHTML=
    result;};
var result = query(SELECT * from MyTable, showResults);
doWhateverElseYouNeed();
```

The preceding code will query the database and move on to the `doWhateverElseYouNeed` function until the query is finished, at which point it will execute the `showResult` callback function. This can be very confusing and make your code difficult to read, but it is very powerful, and on the server side, it allows for a large number of connections.

Now that you have an idea of what Node.js can do, you can download it at `http://nodejs.org/`. Follow the instructions to install Node.js based on your operating system. Once it is installed, you will have a command-line interface and a Node.js window on Windows. Using the command line, you can launch your applications and install additional packages, which you will learn to do in a later example.

A basic Node.js server with Leaflet

In this first example, you will create a simple Node.js server and serve `LeafletEssentials.html`. You can write your code in any text editor and save it as a `.js` file.

Create a folder to store your files and place a copy of `LeafletEssentials.html` in the folder. This will be the file that we are going to serve with Node.js. Next, you will create the server as shown in the following code:

```
require('http').createServer(function (req, res) {
    if ('/' == req.url){
         res.writeHead(200, { 'Content-Type': 'text/html' });
    require('fs').createReadStream('leafletessentials.html')
      .pipe(res);
       }
}).listen(3000);
```

The preceding code uses two modules: `http` and `fs`. You import these modules using `require(module)`. Both of these modules are standard Node.js modules and do not require any additional downloads. The preceding code imports the `http` module and then calls the `createServer()` method. It uses an anonymous function that takes a request and a response—`req` and `res`, respectively. The `if` block tests to see whether the request to the server is equal to the root directory; in this example, whether the browser is pointed to `http://localhost:3000`. The last line of code is listening on port 3000. If the request is to the root directory, then the code writes a header. It is beyond the scope of this book to cover the HTTP protocol and headers. However, know that when a response is sent, it is status 200 if successful and status 404 if it is not successful, and the response has the content type `text/html`. Lastly, the code imports the `fs` module and uses `pipe()` to read in and write out the contents of `LeafletEssentials.html`. Pipe is the preferred method for sending files; however, you could also manually write the HTML as a string using `res.end('the HTML')`. Piping allows you to do some neat things, such as reading and writing out a video file so that the user can play it while it is still receiving data from the server. Writing out HTML as a string will make your code long and complicated; never mind trying to escape all the quotes required in most HTML. In the last example, you will learn about a templating library in which you can store your HTML.

Using the command in tool, navigate to the directory that holds your
server.js code and run it by typing node server.js. Point your browser
to http://localhost:3000. You should see your loaded map as shown:

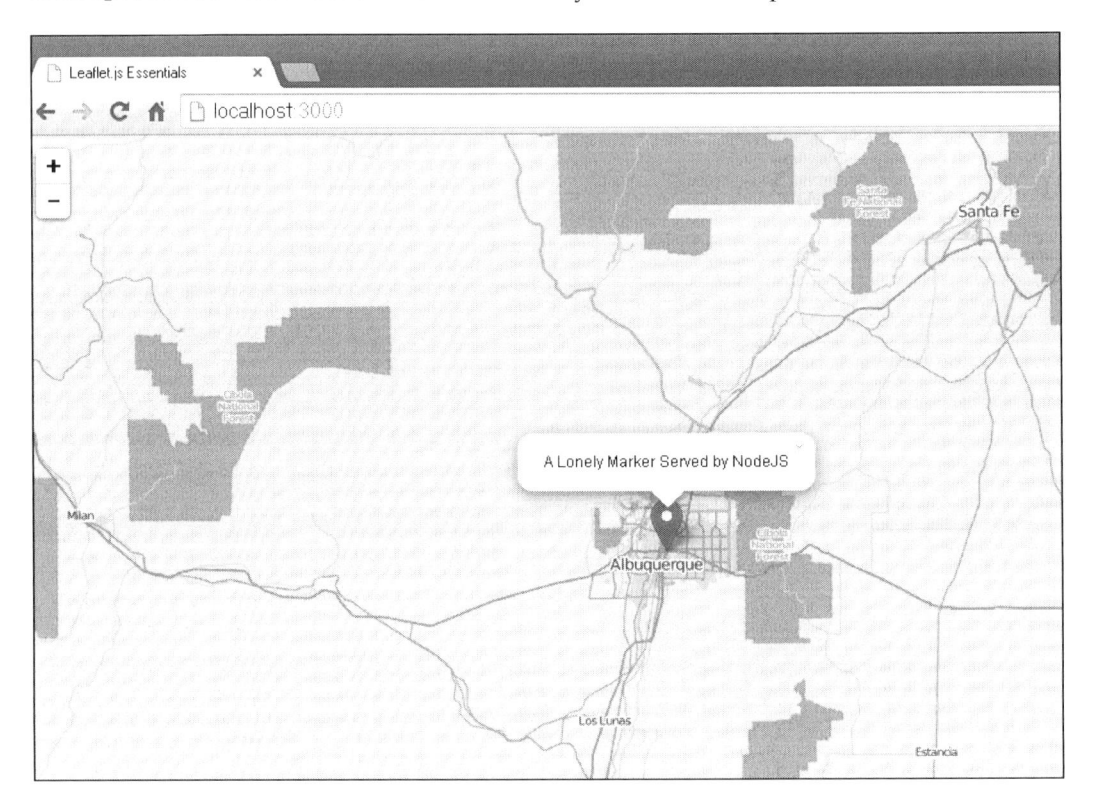

The preceding example simply serves a single file, and if the user points their
browser to any other URL, such as http://localhost:3000/about.html, they
will not see anything, not even an error message. The next example fixes this.

Node.js, AJAX, and Leaflet

Now that you have a Node.js server running and serving up a Leaflet web page, you
can use the same server to make **Asynchronous JavaScript and XML (AJAX)** calls. You
are programming in JavaScript, so even though there is XML in AJAX, you should use
JSON; it is much easier to handle than XML in JavaScript. Building on the first example,
the following code adds another page and sends an error message on bad requests:

```
require('http').createServer(function (req, res) {
  if ('/' == req.url){
        res.writeHead(200, { 'Content-Type': 'text/html' });
```

[130]

```
    require('fs').createReadStream('leafletessentialsAjax.html')
      .pipe(res);
        } else if ('/getpoints'==req.url){
          res.writeHead(200, { 'Content-Type': 'application/json'
            });
          res.end(JSON.stringify([{"lat":35,"long":-106}]));
    } else {
        res.writeHead(404);
        res.end('The page you requested '+req.url+' was not
          found');
    }
}).listen(3000);
```

The preceding code makes two changes to the first example; it adds two new routes. The first `if` statement is the same, returning `LeafletEssentials.html`. The `else if` statement checks to see whether the browser is pointed at http://localhost:3000/getpoints. If it is, then the server returns a JSON string, `[{"lat":35,"long":-106}]`. Lastly, if the user requests a page that doesn't exist, the server will return a 404 error message saying that the page is not found and will return the value of the page they were looking for — `req.url`.

The preceding server requires a change to your `LeafletEssentials.html` file. You will need a subscriber for the `click` event and to make an AJAX call when it occurs. Before AJAX, you will need to submit a form or make a request to the server and then be redirected to a new page that would display the results. AJAX allows you to make a request to the server, have the results returned, and display them without reloading the entire page. In this example, you will make an AJAX call to the `getpoints` URL. You will receive a JSON representation of a point. Then, you will add a marker that will represent the returned point — all without refreshing the web page:

```
map.on('click',function(){
var xhReq = new XMLHttpRequest();
xhReq.open("GET", "getpoints", true);
xhReq.send();
var serverResponse = xhReq.responseText;
var d=JSON.parse(serverResponse);
L.marker([d[0].lat,d[0].long]).addTo(map).bindPopup("Added via
  AJAX call to Node.js").openPopup();
});
```

Without getting too deeply into the details of AJAX, the preceding code creates an `XMLHttpRequest` instance and opens the `getpoints.html` web page.

> For a quick lesson on `XMLHttpRequest`, check out the W3Schools website at http://www.w3schools.com/xml/xml_http.asp.

It then receives the response, parses out the points separated by a comma, and then adds them to the map as a marker. You're only receiving a single point, so the d variable only has a single value, which is represented by d[0]. Objects in JavaScript are used by calling the object and then the value of a field, in this case, d[0].lat and d[0].long.

Your map will look exactly as it did in the first example. When you click on the map, you will see another point, and your map will look like the following screenshot:

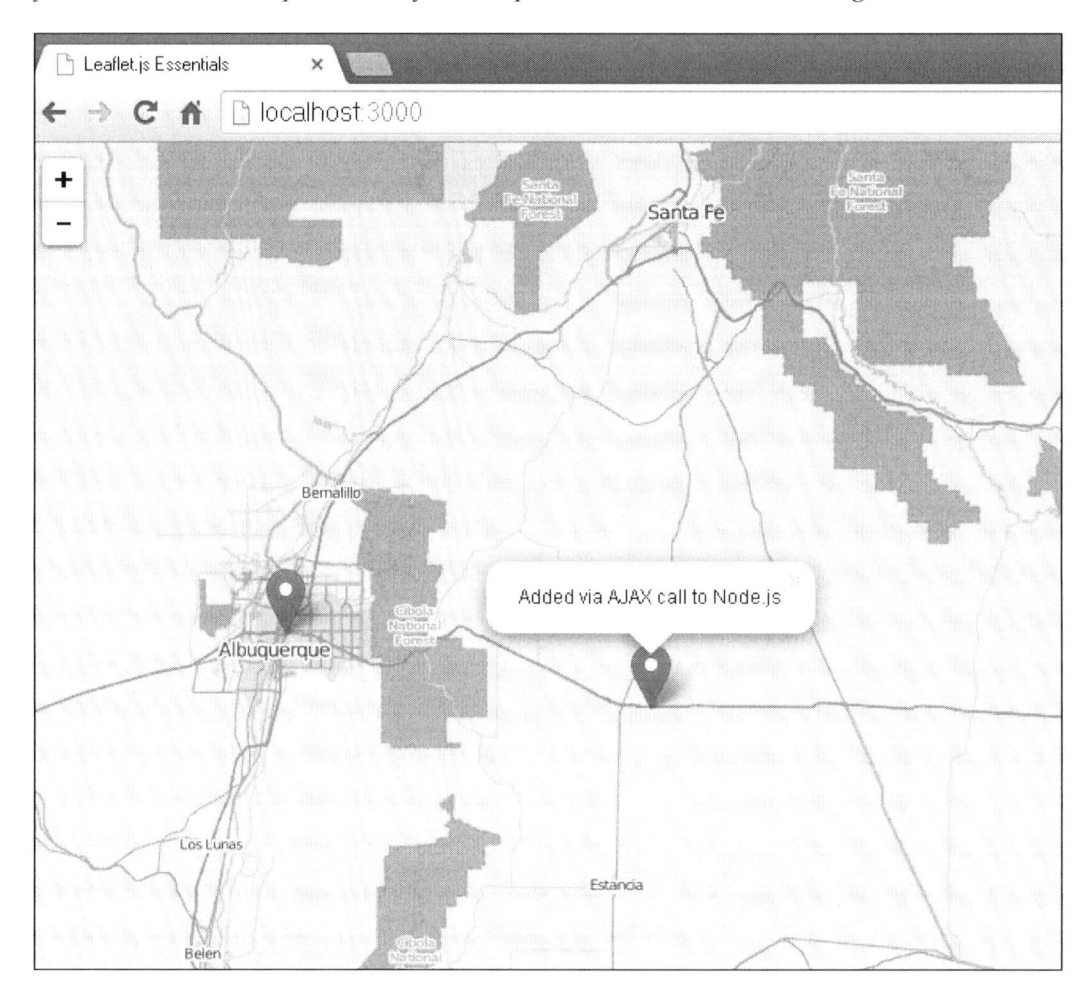

This example returns the same point when the user clicks on the map. This example can be improved by returning a different point every time the user clicks on the map. To do so, simply use a random number generator to return a new latitude and longitude. The key here is to set the maximum and minimum values so that the point is close to our current location. The following code uses `Math.random()` to return different values. To do so, replace the `res.end(JSON.stringify([{"lat":35,"long":-106}]));` line in the server code with the following code:

```
var lat=Math.random()*(36-35)+35;
var lon=Math.random()*(-107+106)-106;
res.end(JSON.stringify([{"lat":lat,"long":lon}]));
```

Now, when the user clicks on the map, the points will appear at random. After several clicks, your map should look like this:

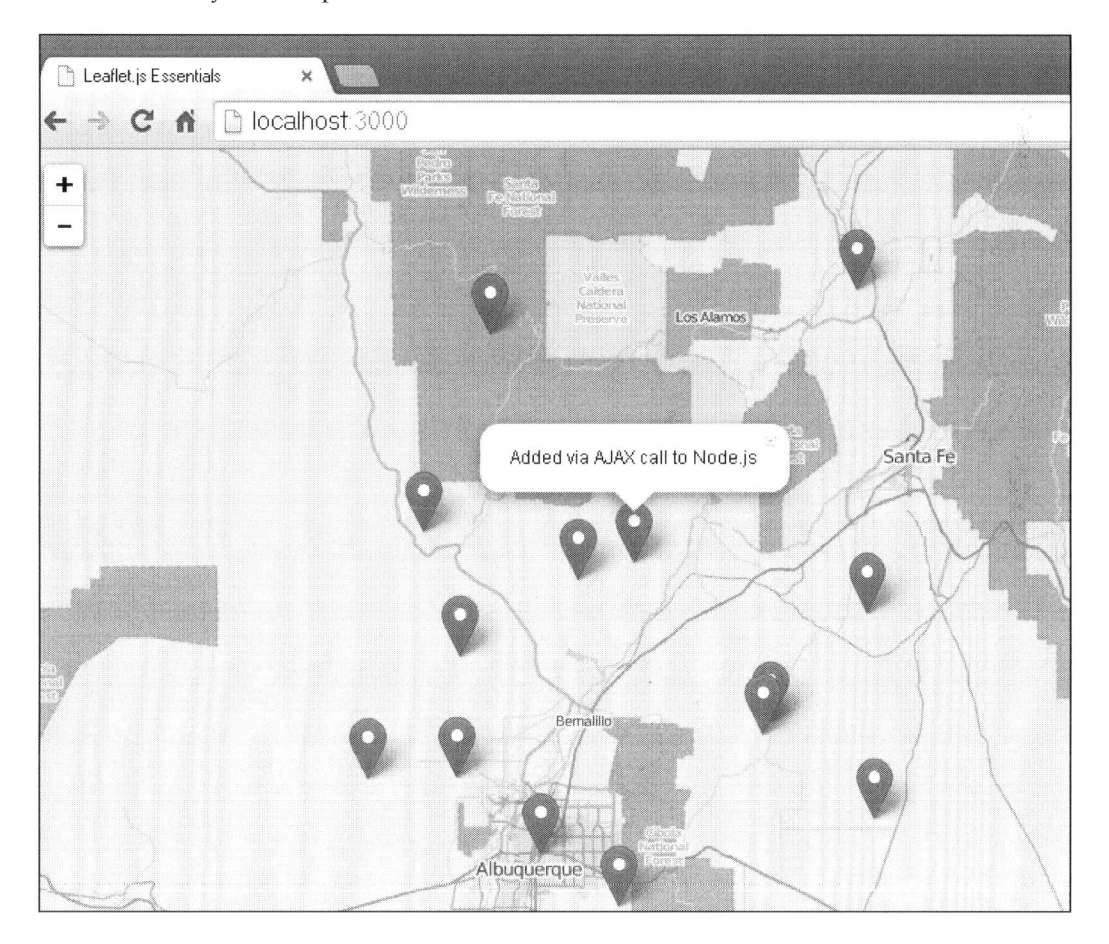

Node.js, Connect, and Leaflet

In the previous example, you had to write the path for every possible URL. A user could type that path in your domain. You allowed two possibilities and sent an error for every other possibility. If you have a website with many pages, you would not want to type an `if` statement for every URL. Connect is a module that provides a middleware code for common tasks. The middleware allows you to accomplish these common tasks with minimal work on your part; you just need to use the `use()` function.

> You can learn about Connect at http://www.senchalabs.org/connect/.

To install Connect, open the command-line tool for Node.js and enter the following command:

`npm install -g connect`

npm is a Node.js package manager. The preceding command launches the package manager and asks it to install Connect. The -g switch is to install it globally so that it is available everywhere on the machine. When Connect is installed, your command prompt will look like this:

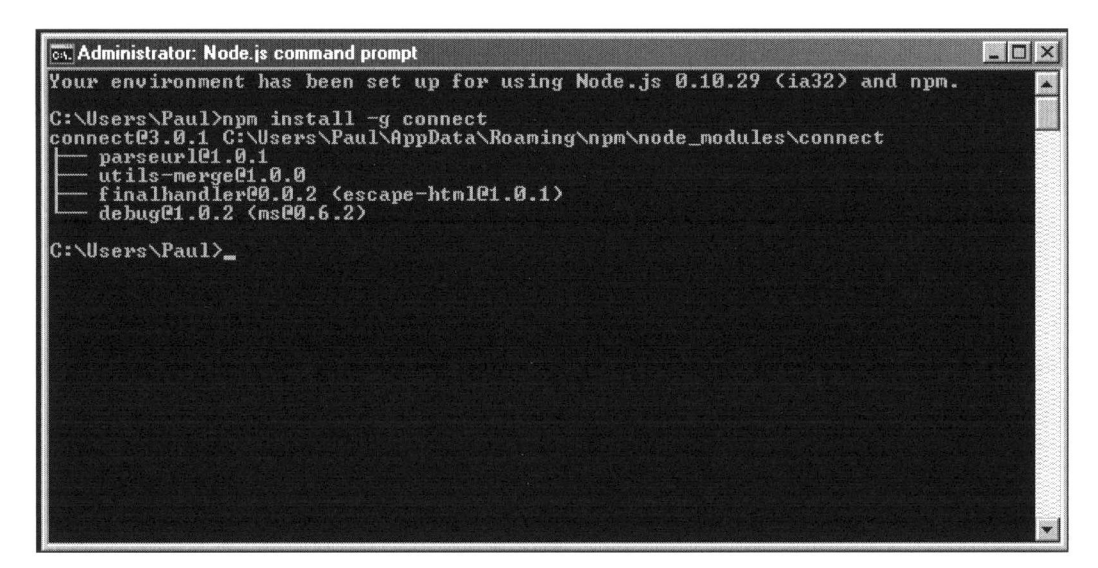

```
Administrator: Node.js command prompt
Your environment has been set up for using Node.js 0.10.29 (ia32) and npm.

C:\Users\Paul>npm install -g connect
connect@3.0.1 C:\Users\Paul\AppData\Roaming\npm\node_modules\connect
├── parseurl@1.0.1
├── utils-merge@1.0.0
├── finalhandler@0.0.2 (escape-html@1.0.1)
└── debug@1.0.2 (ms@0.6.2)

C:\Users\Paul>_
```

> Make note of the version that is installed because you will need this in a later step.

Once you have Connect installed, you can start the example. This example will create a simple server that will only serve static files. Perform the following steps to create the server:

1. Make a `project` folder and place another folder inside and name it www.
2. Place several HTML files in the directory, but especially `LeafletEssentials.html` and `getpoints.json`. You can use the sample included with the book or you can create your own. A minimum `getpoints.json` file would contain the following contents:

   `[{"lat":35,"long":-106}]`

   The contents of the file are a single point represented in JSON. You can add as many points as you like. You can even write a script to update the contents of the file at a set interval.

3. Next, in the main project folder, create a file with the following contents and name it `package.json`. Note that this example is using a version of Connect prior to Version 3:

   ```
   {
   "name": "leafletessentials",
   "version": "0.0.1",
   "dependencies": {"connect": "2.21.1"}
   }
   ```

   This file is used to build the project. At the command line, navigate to your `project` directory and type `npm install`. The package manager will read the `package.json` file and create a new subfolder in your `project` folder named `Node_modules`.

4. Open the folder and you will see another folder with all of the files for the Connect module. Before writing the server, you need to make a change in `LeafletEssentialsAjax.html`. The code for the AJAX call needs to point to the `getpoints.json` file. Now you are ready to write the server.

The first thing to do is to import the Connect module with `require()` and assign it to a variable. Create a server by calling `connect()`. And lastly, invoke the middleware `static()` and ask it to take the www directory and serve all files within it. The `_dirname` variable takes the current directory and concatenates it with the `/www` directory, giving the path to your files as shown in the following code. Listen on any available port:

```
var connect = require('connect')
var server = connect();
server.use(connect.static(__dirname+ '/www'));
server.listen(3000);
```

The code is much shorter than the previous examples. There are no `if ('/' == req.url)` statements. The middleware knows all the files in the directory, and if a URL that matches a filename is requested, it will be sent. If it does not exist, the middleware will send the error page. If you add a new HTML file, it will be served up as soon as it is placed in the folder and requested. Now, when you connect and get your map, you can click on it, and the contents of `getpoints.json` will be returned and displayed on the map.

Node.js, Express, Jade, and Leaflet

In the first two examples, you had to create a static HTML file for the server to serve to the client. In this example, you will use a template that allows you to pass variables to the HTML when loaded. This will allow you to create dynamic data-driven websites.

For this example, you will need to install the Jade module for Node.js. To do so, open the command-line tool and enter the following command. This is the same procedure as the previous example.

```
echo '{}' > package.json
npm install jade -save
```

Now, you have the Jade module installed globally. You will also need to install Express. Express is one of the most popular web frameworks that can be used with Node.js. It is similar to Connect, but in this example, it is the tool that allows us to use a view engine, which is Jade. Again, type the following command and make sure that you note the installed versions:

```
echo '{}' > package.json
npm install express -save
```

> For more information on Express and Jade, you can go to the website for Express at http://expressjs.com/ and for Jade at http://jade-lang.com/.

Now that you have both modules installed, create a folder for your application. In the folder, you will need to create the `package.json` file. In this example, you have two dependencies, so your file should look like the following code:

```
{
"name": "leafletessentials",
"version": "0.0.1",
"dependencies": {
   "express": "4.4.5",
   "jade": "1.3.1"
 }
}
```

Using the command-line tool, navigate to the application directory and use npm to add the dependencies using the following command:

```
npm install
```

You will now have a `Node.js_modules` folder with the `Jade` and `Express` subfolders. You will need a directory to hold or view the template file. This folder needs to be named `views` because that is where Express will look. Create the directory and then open a text editor to create your view. For a quick introduction to Jade, you can read the tutorial at http://jade-lang.com/tutorial/. The important thing to note is that Jade is whitespace sensitive, and hence indentations must be exact. This can be extremely frustrating at first. The following template is the modified `LeafletEssentials.html` file that you have been using in the previous examples. One key difference is the fourth line: `title = title`. This line sets the title of the HTML document to the value of a variable, `title`, in the server code:

```
doctype html
html(lang="en")
    head
        title= title
link(rel='stylesheet', href='http://cdn.leafletjs.com/leaflet-
    0.7.2/leaflet.css')
script(src="http://cdn.leafletjs.com/leaflet-0.7.2/leaflet.js")
    body
    #map(style='width:'+900+'px;'+'height:'+800+'px')
    script(type='text/javascript').
var map = L.map('map', {center: [35.10418, -106.62987], zoom:
    9});
var base = L.tileLayer('http://{s}.tile.osm.org/{z}/{x}/{y}.png').
addTo(map);
L.marker([35.10418, -106.62987]).addTo(map).bindPopup("A Lonely
    Marker").openPopup();
map.on('click',function(){var xhReq = new
    XMLHttpRequest();xhReq.open("GET", "getpoints",
    false);xhReq.send(null);var serverResponse =
    xhReq.responseText;var d=JSON.parse(serverResponse);L.marker
    ([d[0].lat,d[0].long]).addTo(map).bindPopup
    ("Added via AJAX call to Node.js").openPopup();});
```

Save the preceding code in a file named `LeafletEssentials.jade` within your view folder. Now, you are ready to write the server.

> Jade is a popular and powerful template module; however, there are others too. Two others that might be easier to learn at first are HAML at http://haml.info/ and EJS at http://embeddedjs.com/.

The code for the server is as follows:

```
var express=require('express')
var app = express();
app.set('view engine', 'jade');
app.get('/', function(req,res){
   res.render('LeafletEssentials',{title:"Leaflet Essentials"});
   });
app.get('/getpoints', function(req,res){
   res.send([{'lat':35,'long':-106])
});
var server = app.listen(3000);
```

The preceding code imports the Express module and assigns it to a variable. It then creates an app with Express. The view engine defaults to Jade, but if you want to use another, you need the third line to set the appropriate engine. The next lines use `app.get()` to specify the two URLs that our application will return. The first one will return our view and the second is for the AJAX call and returns a point in JSON. In the first AJAX example, you needed to specify `JSON.stringify()` when you returned the point. One of the reasons to use a framework is that it takes care of many common tasks for you. In this case, Express will know what it is you are returning and set the value accordingly. In this example, you are returning a JSON string, and Express will automatically JSONify it for you.

Your map will look just like the one in the previous examples, and when the user clicks, a point will be added. The next examples will use Python to serve a Leaflet application.

Leaflet with Python and CherryPy

The Python programming language is extremely powerful and has a large number of standard libraries and other third-party libraries. It is also fairly easy to pick up for simple tasks. There is extensive documentation, and a large number of books and different libraries are available on the language. You can download Python from the Python website at `https://www.python.org/downloads/`. Version 3 is the latest; however, Version 2.7 is still in use. It is probably best to start learning with Version 3, but if you have v2.7, it will work with the examples.

In this example, you will use the CherryPy library. You can download the library at `http://www.cherrypy.org/`.

> For more books on CherryPy and Python web development, visit `http://www.packtpub.com/CherryPy/book` or `http://www.packtpub.com/python-3-web-development-beginners-guide/book`.

CherryPy is a smaller web framework compared to Django or Pyramid—formerly Pylons. For this example, it will allow you to get up and running quickly without much overhead. To manually install a third-party Python library, extract it to a folder and run the following command:

`python setup.py install`

After running the command, you will be able to import the library in your Python code. For this example, you will connect to a NoSQL database: MongoDB. MongoDB is a document database. It stores everything as a JSON-style document, not in relational tables. While it's not as spatially enabled as PostGIS, which is an extension to PostgreSQL, it has a few spatial features that make it an excellent choice for a Leaflet backend. You can download MongoDB at `http://www.mongodb.org/`.

To use MongoDB with Python, you will also need to download and install PyMongo. You can download the library at `https://pypi.python.org/pypi/pymongo/`. Once you have your environment set up, you can start your MongoDB by running the application mongod.

> If you receive an error about a missing path, you will need to add the `C:\data\db` directory. Just create the folders and then rerun mongod. On Linux and OS X, execute `mkdir -p /data/db` to add the data directory.

Your database is empty. The pa.py Python file that is available on these books' website will create a database and populate it with the public art data that was used in earlier chapters of this book. The file looks like the following code:

```
from pymongo import Connection
from pymongo import GEO2D
db=Connection().albuquerque
db.publicart.create_index([("loc",GEO2D)])
db.publicart.insert({"loc":[35.1555,-106.591838],"name":"Almond
  Blossom/Astronomy","popup":
  http://farm8.staticflickr.com/7153/6831137393_fa38634fd7_m.jpg
  })
  db.publicart.insert({"loc":[35.0931,-106.664177],
  "name":"Formas Esperando Palabra de Otros
  Mundos","popup":
"http://farm3.staticflickr.com/2167/2479129916_0d861b2600.jpg"})
print " Completed..."
```

Leaflet in Node.js, Python, and C#

The preceding code imports two modules from the PyMongo library: Connection and GEO2D. The first handles our connection to the DB and the second allows us to spatially enable it. The next line makes a connection to a database called `albuquerque`. Next, a spatially enabled index is created for a collection called `publicart` and it indexes the `loc` field. The next two lines are public art points that are inserted into the collection. They each contain a location, name, and pop-up field that contains the URL to an image of the piece.

Execute the file by typing `python pa.py`. Your MongoDB will now have a database, collection, and enough data to allow you to try some samples.

> If you ever delete, corrupt, or just want to refresh your database, you can run this file over again to start a fresh.

Now that you have your database running and populated and have Python installed with CherryPy and PyMongo, you are now ready to write your first server:

1. The first step is to import the Python libraries as follows:

   ```
   import cherrypy
   from pymongo import Connection,GEO2D
   ```

2. Next, you create a class and a function that will represent the URL to your application. In this example, it will be the `index` function:

   ```
   class mongocherry(object):
       def index(self):
   ```

3. The function will first create an array to hold the contents of an HTML file. You can append the contents of `LeafletEssentials.html` up until you add the tile layer basemap:

   ```
   output =[]

   output.append("<HTML><HEAD><TITLE>QUERY
     MONGODB</TITLE></HEAD><BODY><h1>Query MongoDB</h1><link
     rel='stylesheet' href='http://cdn.leafletjs.com/leaflet-
     0.7.2/leaflet.css' /><style> html, body, #map {padding:
     0;margin: 0;height: 100%;}</style></head><body><script
     src='http://cdn.leafletjs.com/leaflet-
     0.7.2/leaflet.js'></script><div
     id='map'></div><script>var map = L.map('map',{center:
     [35.10418, -106.62987],zoom:
     9});L.tileLayer
   ('http://{s}.tile.osm.org/{z}/{x}/{y}.png').addTo(map);")
   ```

[140]

4. Now, create the database connection and search for all documents in the collection named `publicart`. The `find()` function will return a large number of records. On each record, you will append an HTML string, creating a marker using the record. The location field creates the marker and the name and pop-up fields are added to the markers' pop up:

```
db=Connection().albuquerque
for x in db.publicart.find():
    output.append("L.marker(["+str(x["loc"][0])+","+str(x["loc"
      ][1])+"]).addTo(map).bindPopup(\""+x["name"]+"<img
      src='"+x["popup"]+"'>\");")
```

5. Once all the documents are added, you can append the closing HTML tags to the array. Then, convert the array to a string so that you can return it when the user requests the index of the application as follows:

```
output.append('</SCRIPT></BODY></HTML>')
i=0
html=""
while i<len(output):
    html+=str(output[i])
    i+=1
return html
```

6. Lastly, you need to expose the `index` function, set the address and port the application will use, and then start the server by calling the classname:

```
index.exposed = True
cherrypy.config.update({'server.socket_host': '127.0.0.1',
'server.socket_port': 8000,
})
cherrypy.quickstart(mongocherry())
```

When you have finished, run the program by opening a command line and typing the following command:

python mongocherry.py

Open a browser and point it to `http://127.0.0.1:8000`. You should see a map like the following one:

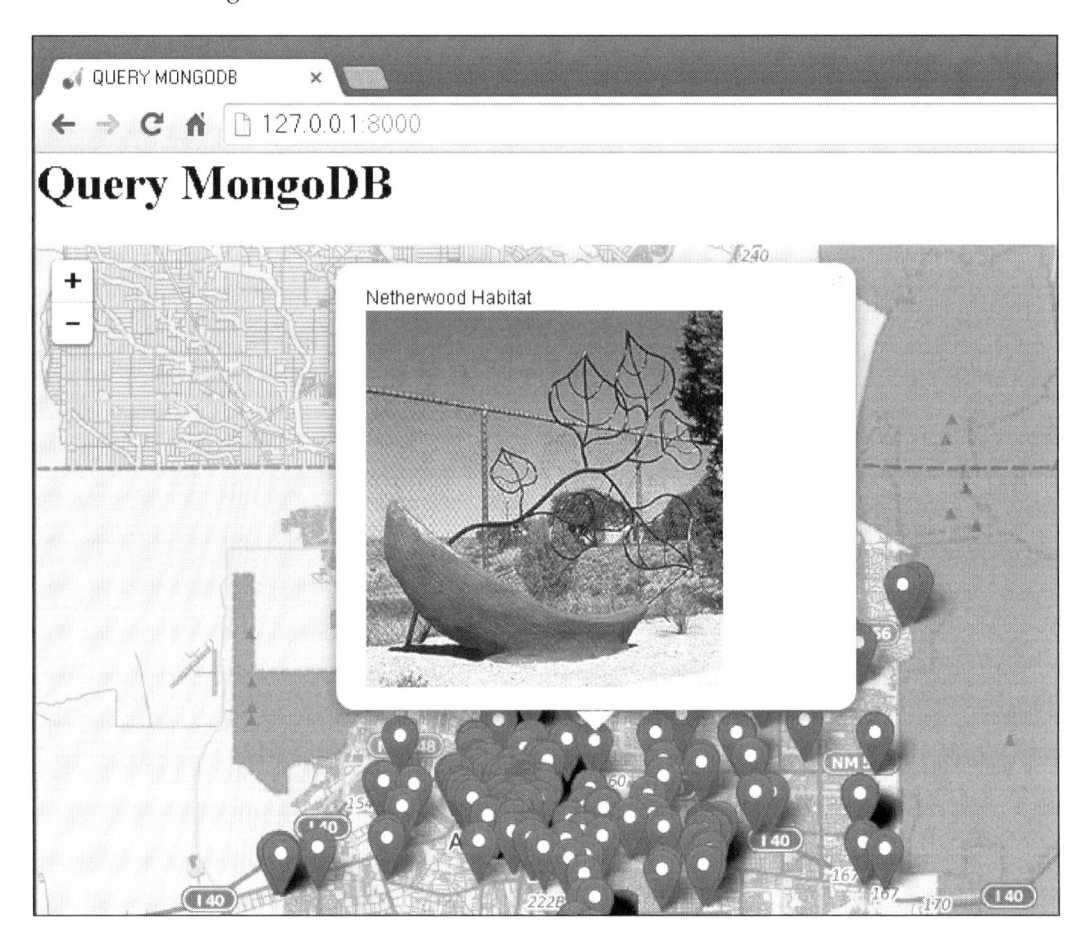

The application returned the contents of your MongoDB and displayed them in a Leaflet map. Now that you know how to create a URL route in an application, let's expand on this example to add an AJAX call for spatial searches.

Spatial queries with Python, MongoDB, and Leaflet

MongoDB allows you to access spatial queries. You can search for results near a single point, near a point by setting a maximum distance, within a bounding rectangle, or within a circle. In this example, you will query for results near a point.

Import the required libraries. In the following code, you will import two new module tools from the `cherrypy` library and `json`:

```
import cherrypy
from pymongo import Connection,GEO2D
from cherrypy import tools
import json
```

After importing the libraries, perform the following steps:

1. Create the class. Using tools, you will expose the function with the @ sign. Connect to the database and write out the HTML code. The HTML code in this example is different. You will add a listener for the `click` event. The code for this block will make an AJAX call to the `getdata` page and pass it the `(x,y)` coordinates of the `click` event. The data returned will only contain three objects, so you can hardcode the HTML instead of running a `for` loop as follows:

```
class mongocherry(object):
    @cherrypy.expose
    def index(self):
        db=Connection().albuquerque
        output =[]
    output.append("<HTML><HEAD><TITLE>QUERY
MONGODB</TITLE></HEAD><BODY><h1>Query MongoDB</h1><link
rel='stylesheet' href='http://cdn.leafletjs.com/leaflet-
0.7.2/leaflet.css' /><style> html, body, #map {padding:
0;margin: 0;height: 100%;}</style></head><body><script
src='http://cdn.leafletjs.com/leaflet-
0.7.2/leaflet.js'></script><div id='map'></div><script>var
lat; var lon; var map = L.map('map',{center: [35.10418, -
106.62987],zoom:
9});L.tileLayer('http://{s}.tile.osm.org/{z}/{x}/{y}.png')
.addTo(map);map.on('click',function(e){var
a=String(e.latlng).split(\",\");lat=a[0].split(\"(\");lon=a
[1].split(\")\");var xhReq = new XMLHttpRequest();var
s=\"getdata?x=\";var s2=String(lat[1]);var s3=\"&y=\";var
s4=String(lon[0]);var url=s.concat(s2,s3,s4);
xhReq.open(\"GET\", url, false); xhReq.send(null); var
serverResponse = xhReq.responseText; var
d=JSON.parse(serverResponse);L.marker([d[0].lat,d[0].long])
.addTo(map);L.marker([d[1].lat,d[1].long]).addTo(map);L.mar
ker([d[2].lat,d[2].long]).addTo(map);});")
```

2. Next, close the HTML tags, convert them to a string, and return them when the `page` function is called:

   ```
   output.append("</SCRIPT></BODY></HTML>")
   i=0
   html=""
   while i<len(output):
           html+=str(output[i])
           i+=1


   return html
   ```

3. Now, you will define and expose another URL function. This one will be called `getdata` and it will handle the AJAX call from the users' click. This function gets passed the `x` and `y` variables. These will be the coordinates of the users' click. The query in this example is different than the previous example. Notice that you use `find()` but add `$near` and pass it the coordinates of the users' click. The search is set to only return three results. Lastly, you pass back the results as JSON using `@tools.json_out()`, as follows:

   ```
    @cherrypy.expose
    @tools.json_out()
    def getdata(self,x,y):
   db=Connection().albuquerque
   data=[]
   lat=float(x)
   long=float(y)
   for doc in db.publicart.find({"loc": {"$near": [lat,
     long]}}).limit(3):
     data.append({'lat':str(doc["loc"][0]),'long':
       str(doc["loc"][1])})
    return data
   ```

4. Lastly, set the IP address of the server and port. Then, run it:

   ```
   cherrypy.config.update({'server.socket_host': '127.0.0.1',
                           'server.socket_port': 8000,
                          })
   cherrypy.quickstart(mongocherry())
   ```

Now you can run the file and point your browser to `http://127.0.0.1:8000`. You will see a blank map. Click anywhere on the map and you will see three points appear. These are the closest points to where you clicked. Your map will look like the following screenshot after clicking once:

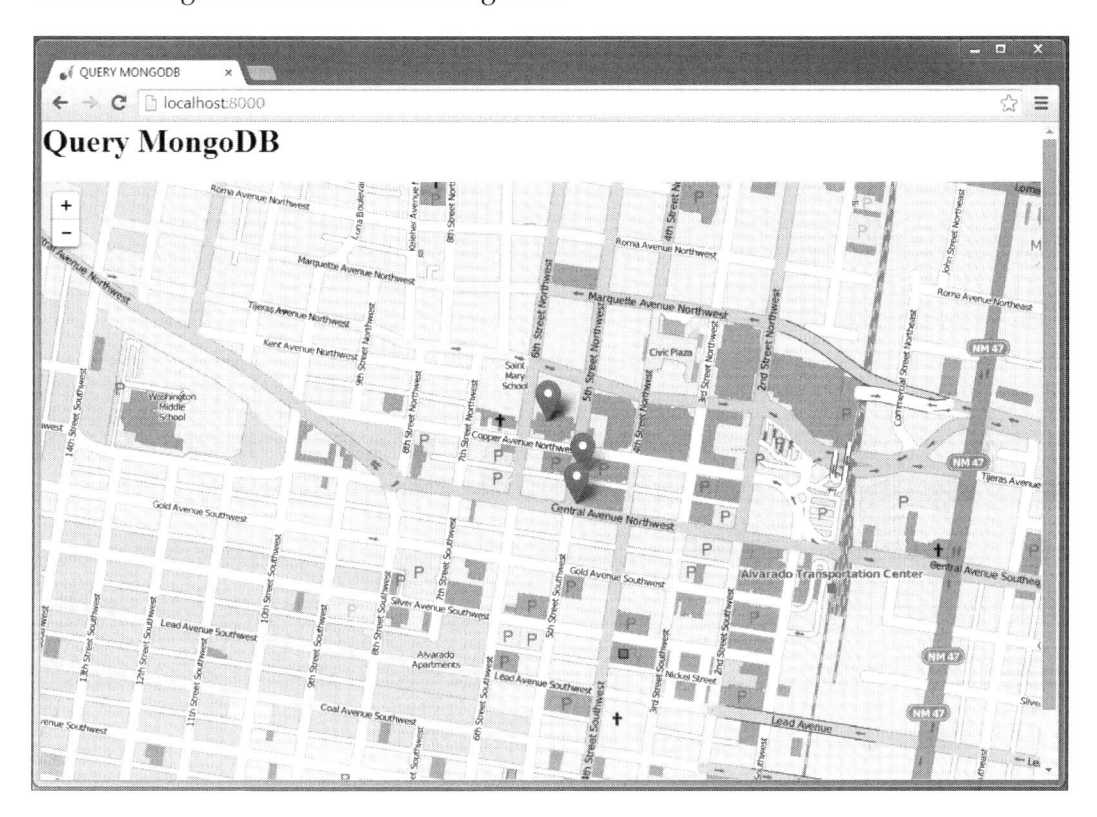

Using Python to connect to your MongoDB allows you to not only query the database to display results, but with a little more code, you can use it to save the results of a map. You could allow the user to click on the map where they would like to add a point and then use the `(x,y)` coordinates and perform an `insert()` method instead of a `find()` function. The preceding examples provided a very brief overview of how to serve up a Leaflet map with Python and handle AJAX queries. The next examples will move on to using C# to make desktop applications with Leaflet.

Desktop applications in C# with Leaflet

Leaflet is used in a web page; however, with C#, you can embed a web browser in a Windows form to create what appears to be a desktop application. The examples in this section will show you how to add a map to a C# application, add a point by calling a JavaScript function from C#, and show you how to connect to MongoDB in C# and display the results on the map.

Adding a map to a C# application

To build an application in C#, you will need to install Microsoft Visual Studio Express. You will need at least Visual Studio C# 2010. You can download it at http://www.visualstudio.com/downloads/download-visual-studio-vs. This program is a slimmed-down version of the commercial Visual Studio. It allows you to rapidly build **Windows Form Applications** and compile your code in to an easily redistributable Windows Executable.

Launch the application and create a new **Windows Form Application** from the dialog box, as shown in the following screenshot:

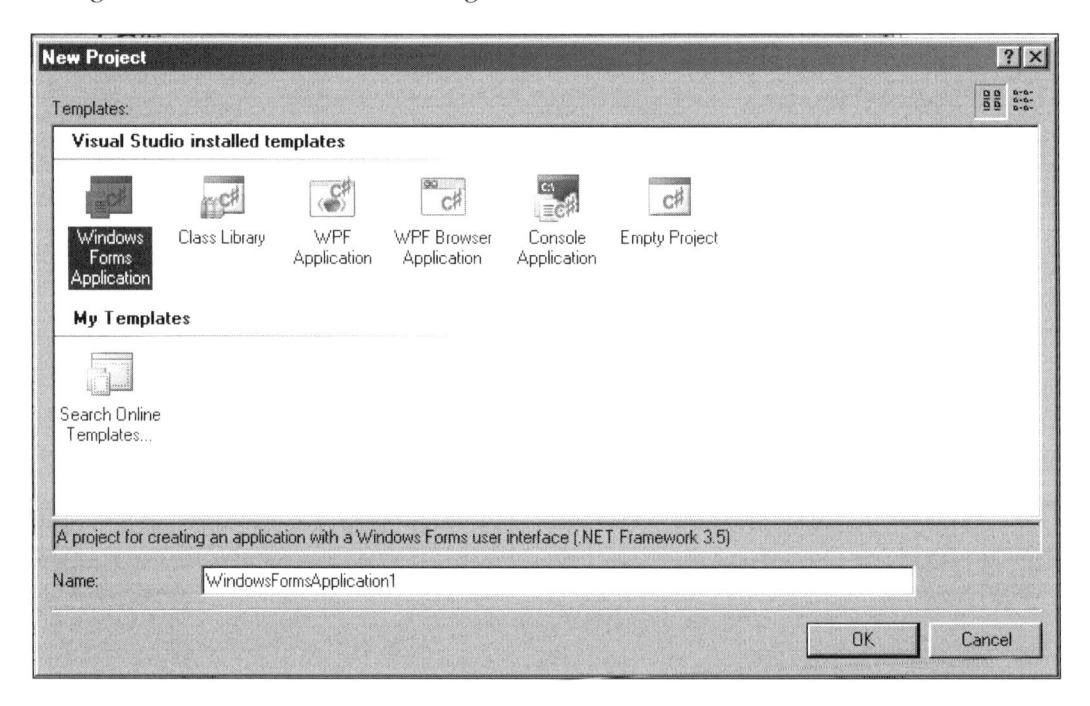

Chapter 6

Your application will be a blank form. Select the toolbox on the upper-left corner of the window and drag the web browser to the form, as shown in the following screenshot:

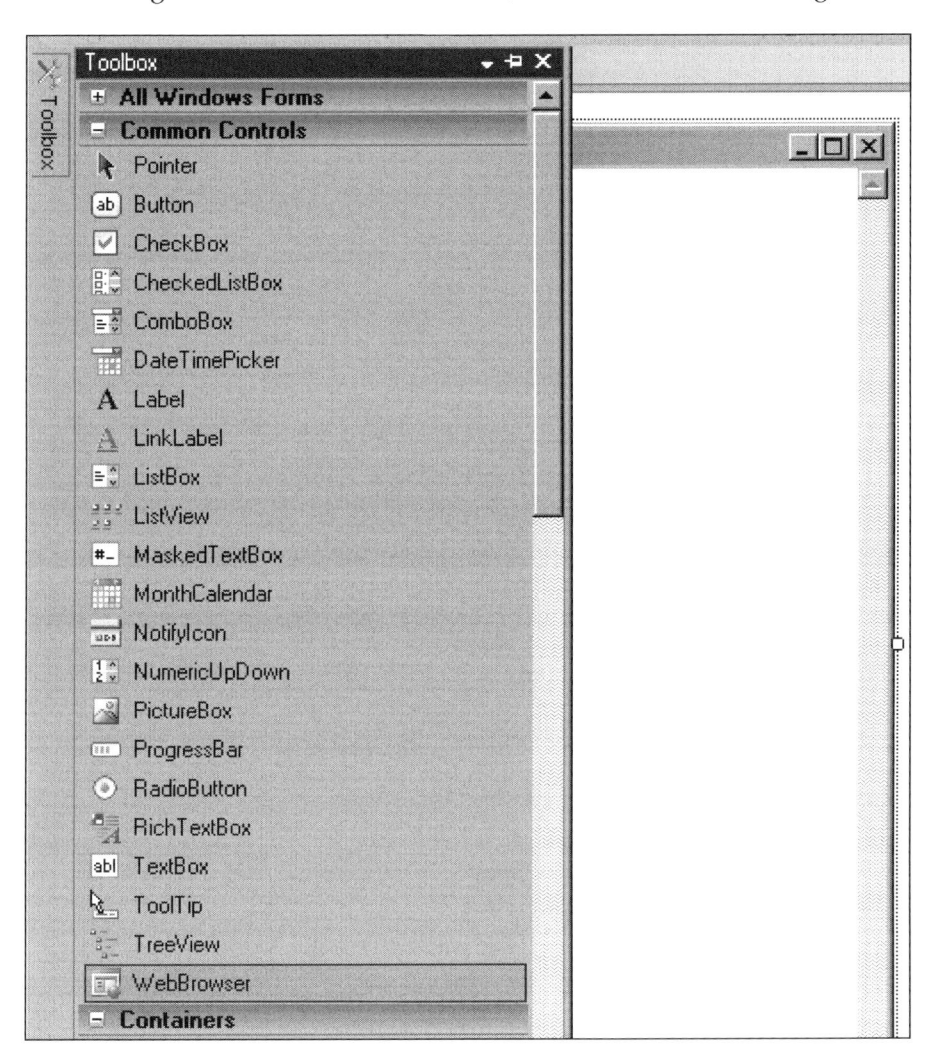

Click on the web browser that you dragged to the form and modify the URL property to point to an instance of LeafletEssentials.html running on your web server. Save the application. Click on the **Debug** menu and then start debugging. Your application will launch and you will see your Leaflet map loaded in the Windows Form, as shown in the following screenshot:

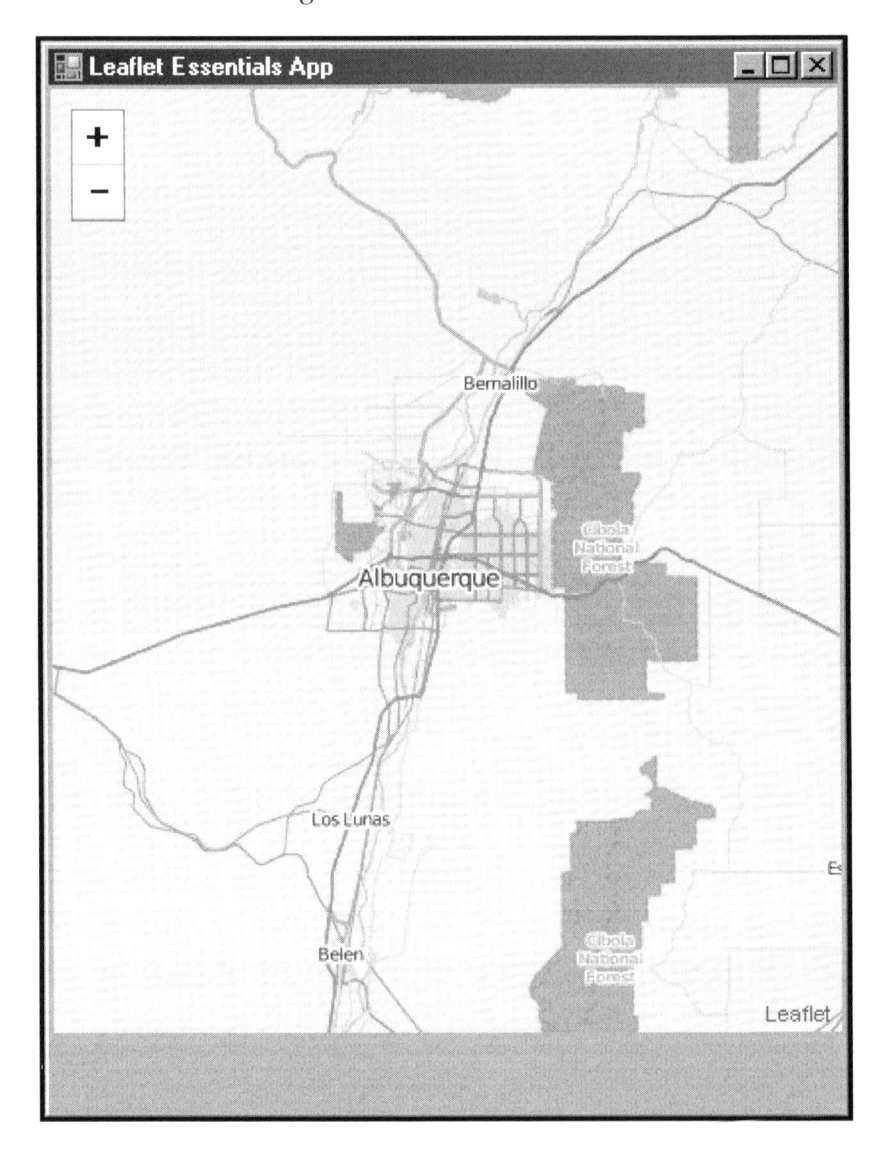

You now have a map in a C# application without any code. The next example will add some functionality to your application.

Adding a marker in C#

In this example, you will build on the previous example by adding a marker. The first thing you need to do is drag a button onto the bottom of the form using the toolbox. In the properties of the button, change the `text` property from `button1` to `Add Marker`. Then, double-click on the button.

You are now looking at the code that Visual Studio created for you when you created the application, and it has now added a function to handle the button click. It wrote the function when you clicked on the button. Before you code the button, you will need to add a reference to `MSHTML.dll`. This file will allow you to use the web and HTML objects you need to make your map work. At the top of your code, you will see several lines that start with `using`. This is where you import the required libraries into your application. The most common ones have already been added. At the end of the list, type the code `using MSHTML;`. It will be underlined and won't be found. You now need to right-click on the project in the **Solution Explorer** window and select **Add Reference**. Add a COM reference to Microsoft HTML Object Library as shown in the following screenshot:

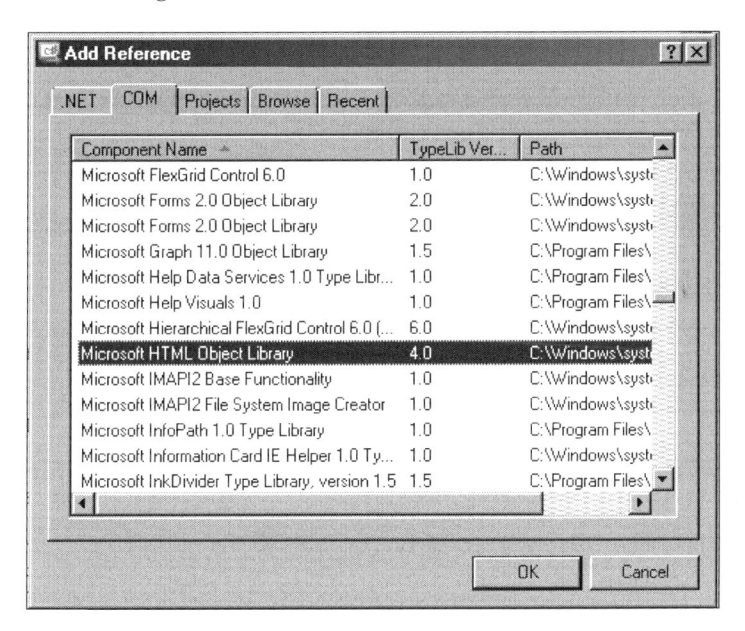

Now that you have added the reference, the underline will disappear and you can start coding the `button1_Click()` function. Add the following code to the function:

```
HtmlElement head = webBrowser1.Document.GetElementsByTagName("head")
[0];
HtmlElement scriptEl = webBrowser1.Document.CreateElement("script");
IHTMLScriptElement element = (IHTMLScriptElement)scriptEl.DomElement;
```

```
element.text = "var mymarker; function addPoints() { mymarker =
new L.marker([36.104743, -106.629925]); map.addLayer(mymarker);
mymarker.bindPopup('HELLO <br>Added By C#.'); }";
head.AppendChild(scriptEl);
webBrowser1.Document.InvokeScript("addPoints");
```

The preceding code grabs the `<head>` tag of the `LeafletEssentials.html` file that you loaded through the web browser properties. It then creates a `<script>` element so that you can add JavaScript to the HTML and execute it. You then create the script element and pass it a `text` string. The string is a JavaScript function for adding a point to the map.

You must wrap your code in a function, because that is how C# will call and execute it. You then append the `<script>` tag to the `<head>` tag of the document and tell the web browser to invoke the `addPoints()` function. So now, when the user clicks on the button, the JavaScript function will be added to `LeafletEssentials.html` and will be executed. Save and debug the project. When the application launches, click on the button and your application should look like this:

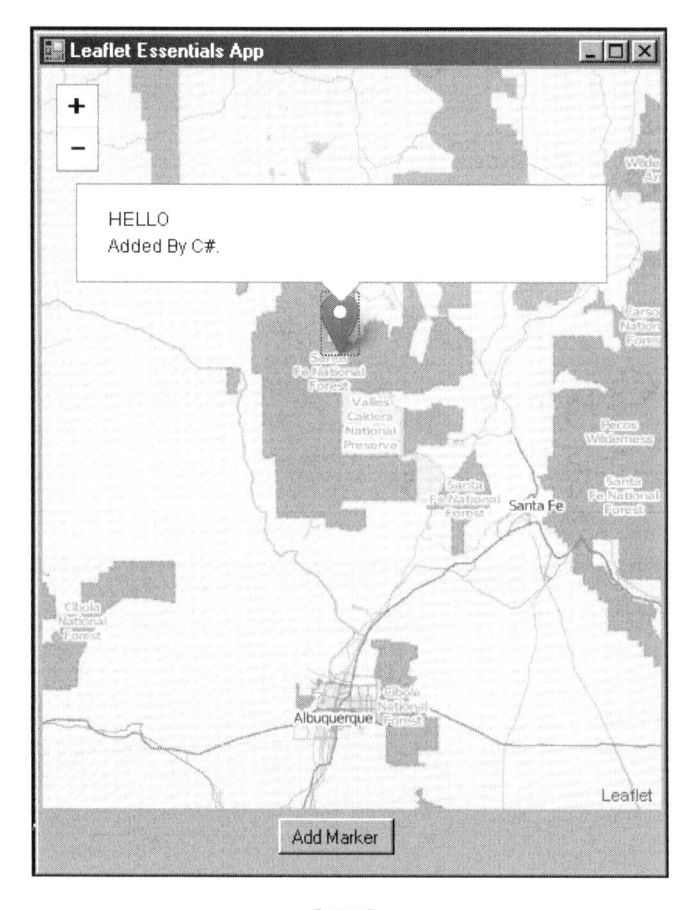

To allow C# applications to modify a Leaflet application, insert a JavaScript function to a base HTML file and then execute it using an event such as a button click. The next example will connect to MongoDB.

Using MongoDB with C# and Leaflet

Just as in the Python example, to use MongoDB in C# will require a driver. You can download the C# drivers at `https://github.com/mongodb/mongo-csharp-driver/releases`. This example uses the `.zip` file. In your project, add another reference, but instead of selecting COM, this time, you will browse to where you extracted the drivers from the `.zip` file. The folder should contain `MongoDB.Bson.dll` and `MongoDB.Driver.dll`. After adding the reference, you must import the required libraries using the following code:

```
using MongoDB.Bson;
using MongoDB.Driver;
using MongoDB.Driver.Linq;
using MongoDB.Driver.Builders;
```

With the libraries imported, you can modify your button to connect to MongoDB and load the points. The following instructions will walk you through the code to connect to MongoDB:

1. First, you will need a string to hold the JavaScript function that will add the points. In C#, you will use `StringBuilder()` so that you can append to the string. You can start by appending the function name and the first brace:

   ```
   StringBuilder myString = new StringBuilder();
   myString.Append("function addPoints() {");
   ```

2. Next, you set up the connection to MongoDB. Connect to the IP and port—the default is localhost on port 27017. Get the server and then the database named `albuquerque`. Lastly, connect to the `publicart` collection:

   ```
   var client = new MongoClient("mongodb://localhost:27017");
   var server = client.GetServer();
   var database = server.GetDatabase("albuquerque");
   var collection = database.GetCollection("publicart");
   ```

3. Now, you can execute the query. The query will find all documents and return each one. The code appends a string, which creates a marker by concatenating the location, name, and pop-up information from each document:

   ```
   foreach (var document in collection.FindAll())
   {
       myString.Append("L.marker([" + document["loc"][0] + "," + document["loc"][1] + "]).addTo(map).bindPopup(\"" + document["name"] + "<br><img src='" + document["popup"] + "'>\");" + "\r\n");
   }
   ```

4. Close the string with the last brace:

```
myString.Append("}");
```

5. The last code block is the same as the previous example. Create the HTML elements and insert the string by converting `StringBuilder.toString()`:

```
HtmlElement head = webBrowser1.Document.
GetElementsByTagName("body")[0];
HtmlElement scriptElement = webBrowser1.Document.
CreateElement("script");
IHTMLScriptElement addPointsElement = (IHTMLScriptElement)
scriptElement.DomElement;
addPointsElement.text = myString.ToString();
head.AppendChild(scriptElement);
webBrowser1.Document.InvokeScript("addPoints");
```

Save and debug the project. When the application is launched, click on the button, and your application should look like the following screenshot:

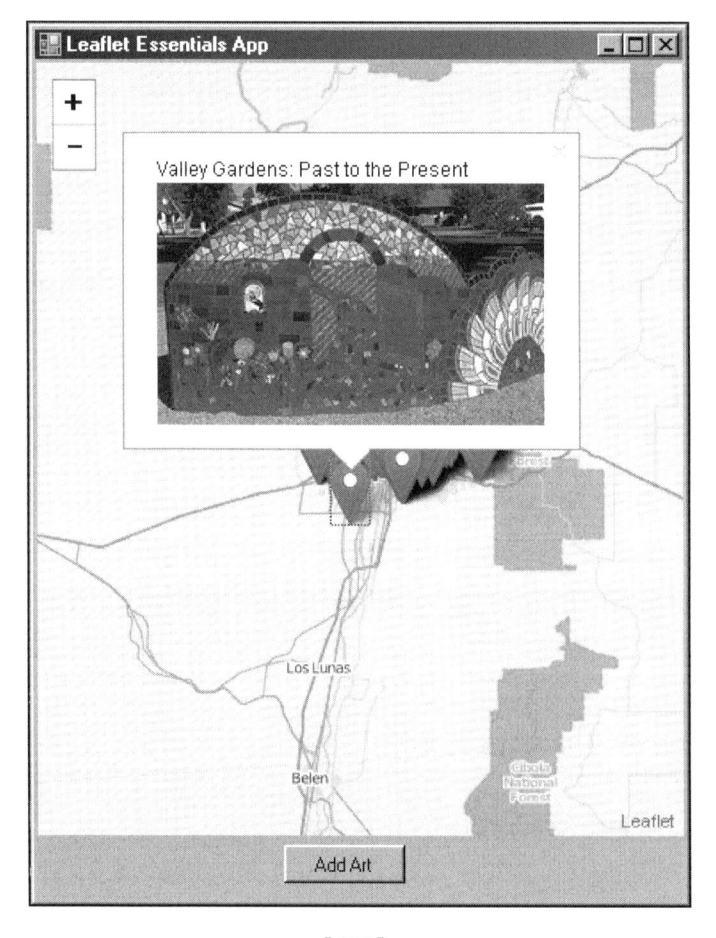

The very last step is to select the `debug` menu and, instead of debugging, select `build solution`. If you browse to the `project` folder, you will have a directory named `bin`. Within the directory, you now have an `.exe` file.

Now, you have a MongoDB collection in a Leaflet map written in C# and compiled as `.exe`. For this to run on another machine, you would only need to make your MongoDB sit on a real IP and allow access from outside your network.

The last example will allow the user to click on the map and return the closest points.

Querying with C#, Leaflet, and MongoDB

You have learned how to pass data from C# to Leaflet by writing a JavaScript function, injecting it into the HTML file, and then executing it. Passing data from JavaScript back to C# is a little different. One way in which you can pass data is to have the JavaScript write the contents to `<div>`, and then C# can read it in. The key here is to set the `<div>` tag to be invisible. The following steps will walk you through the last example:

1. First, modify `LeafletEssentials.html` by adding a new `<div>`, and set the style so that the display is set to `none`. If you set it as `hidden`, it will take up space in the document and there would be a blank spot below your map:

   ```
   <style>
     html, body, #map {
         padding: 0;
         margin: 0;
         height: 100%;
     }
   #points.hidden {
       display: none;
   }
   </style>
   <body>
   <div id="map"></div>
   <div id="points"></div>
   ```

2. Next, create a listener for the `click` event and write a function that creates a marker, showing you the location of the `click` event that cleans up the text of the returned latitude and longitude and writes the results to `<div>`:

   ```
   map.on('click',function(e){L.marker(e.latlng).addTo(map).bi
   ndPopup("SEARCH LOCATION").openPopup();
   var a=String(e.latlng).split(",");
   var lat=a[0].split("(");
   var lon=a[1].split(")");
   document.getElementById("points").innerHTML =
      lat[1]+","+lon[0];
   });
   ```

[153]

Leaflet in Node.js, Python, and C#

3. With the HTML file ready, you can now modify the C#. The first step is to read in the points from the `<div>` tag and then parse them so that each is in its own variable as follows:

   ```
   string hiddenHTML = webBrowser1.Document.GetElementById("points").InnerHtml;
   string[] thePoints = hiddenHTML.Split(',');
   ```

4. Set up the connection to MongoDB. Connect to the IP and port. Get the server and then the database named `albuquerque`. Lastly, connect to the `publicart` collection:

   ```
   var client = new MongoClient("mongodb://localhost:27017");
   var server = client.GetServer();
   var database = server.GetDatabase("albuquerque");
   var collection = database.GetCollection("publicart");
   ```

5. Create a text string of the query and initialize your `StringBuilder()` function to hold the JavaScript of the function and results:

   ```
   var query = Query.Near("loc", double.Parse(thePoints[0]), double.Parse(thePoints[1]));
   StringBuilder myLocString = new StringBuilder();
   myLocString.Append("function addLocPoints() {");
   ```

6. Execute the query in a loop using the `near()` function. Pass the results to the string, building up the JavaScript function:

   ```
               foreach (BsonDocument item in collection.Find(query).SetLimit(5))
               {
                   BsonElement loc = item.GetElement("loc");
                   string g = loc.Value.ToString();
                   string x = g.Trim(new Char[] { '[', ']' });
                   String[] a = x.Split(',');

                   myLocString.Append("L.marker([" + a[0] + "," + a[1] + "]).addTo(map).bindPopup(\"" + item["name"] + "<br><img src='" + item["popup"] + "'>\");" + "\r\n");
               }
   ```

7. The last code block is the same as the previous two examples. Create the HTML elements and insert the string by converting `StringBuilder.toString()`:

   ```
   myLocString.Append("}");
   HtmlElement head = webBrowser1.Document.GetElementsByTagName("body")[0];
   ```

Chapter 6

```
HtmlElement scriptElement = webBrowser1.Document.
CreateElement("script");
IHTMLScriptElement addPointsElement = (IHTMLScriptElement)
scriptElement.DomElement;
addPointsElement.text = myLocString.ToString();
head.AppendChild(scriptElement);
webBrowser1.Document.InvokeScript("addLocPoints");
```

8. Save and debug the project. When the application is launched, click on the button, and your application should look like the following screenshot:

Summary

In this last chapter, you have learned how to use Leaflet.js in other programming languages and frameworks. Starting with Node.js, you learned how to use JavaScript on the frontend and the backend. You created a Node.js server that returned a Leaflet web page. You then modified the code to allow AJAX calls back to the server to update the map without reloading the page.

You also learned how to create a server and allow AJAX requests using Python and CherryPy. The Python example introduced NoSQL databases, in particular, MongoDB. You learned how to write a query to return all the documents in a database collection as well as how to use AJAX to query only points that are near the points where a user has clicked.

Lastly—for something totally different—you learned how to embed a web browser into a Windows Form and run a desktop application with Leaflet. The applications used buttons on the form to execute JavaScript functions that were injected into the LeafletEssentials.html file. You then passed data in the other direction—from JavaScript back to C#—capturing mouse clicks on the map and using them to query MongoDB and return the results. The C# applications you built can then be compiled in a .exe file and distributed to anyone who can connect to your MongoDB and LeafletEssentials.html file.

Index

Symbols

<div> tag
  creating 9
-g switch 134
.join() method 112

A

addLatLng() method, Leaflet.heat 61
addresses
  finding, point used 121
  geocoding, in Leaflet 117
addTo() method 30
alert() function 35
animated heatmap
  creating 67, 68
ArcServer 107
Asynchronous JavaScript and XML (AJAX) 130
attribute query
  creating 122, 123

B

bar chart markers
  creating, with Leaflet Data Visualization Framework 103-105
basemap
  <div> tag, creating 9
  creating, with Leaflet 8
  CSS files, referencing 8
  data, adding to 18
  JavaScript, referencing 8
  map object, creating 10
  points, adding to 19, 20
  polygons, adding to 22
  polylines, adding to 21
  tile layer, adding 10, 11
basic markers
  MapMarker 101, 102
  RegularPolygonMarker 101-103
  StarMarker 101, 103
bindPopup() method 31
blur value, heatmap
  changing 58-60

C

C#
  application, building 146, 148
  map, adding 148
  marker, adding 149-151
  MongoDB, using with 151-153
  querying with 153-155
Cascading Style Sheet. *See* **CSS**
CherryPy
  about 139
  URL 138
  used, for building Leaflet applications 138-142
choropleth map, creating with Leaflet
  about 69
  color, setting 71
  GeoJSON data, adding 70
  GeoJSON data, styling 71, 72
circles
  about 23
  creating 24, 25
clustering, markers
  with Leaflet.markercluster 90

cluster map
  coding 90-92
color
  setting, with function 71
Color Brewer
  URL 71
Color Brewer 2 tool
  URL 60
Connect
  installing 134
  URL 134
  using 135
CSS
  used, for mobile mapping 32, 34
custom function, events
  creating 38
custom marker
  creating 77
  creating, in Leaflet 82, 83
  image, creating in GIMP 78
  image, drawing 79
  image, saving 79
  image, using as icon 81, 82
  L.Icon class, defining 84, 85
  shadow image, creating 80

D

data, adding to basemap
  points 19, 20
  polygons 22
  polylines 21
density map 55
desktop application, C#
  creating, with Leaflet 146
  map, adding 146-148
  marker, adding 149-151
  MongoDB, using 151-153
detectRetina option 109

E

Economic and Social Research Institute. *See* **ESRI**
EJS
  URL 137
ESRI
  about 107

api-reference 114
basemaps 108
ESRI basemaps
  about 108
  label layers 108
  layers 108
  using 108, 109
esri-leaflet-geocoder
  URL 117
esri-leaflet plugin
  used, for creating heatmap 115, 116
ESRI services
  consuming 113, 114
event handler
  events, assigning to 36-38
events
  custom function, creating 38
  handling 36-38
  subscribing 37
Express
  URL 136
Extensible Markup Language (XML) 41

F

feature group 30
features, GeoJSON
  iterating through 50
fillColor option 71
Font Awesome markers
  URL, for downloading 88
  using 88, 89

G

geocoding
  about 117
  from address, to point 117-119
  URL parameters 119, 120
  used, for creating map 117
GeoJSON
  about 42
  history 41
  layers, styling 48-50
  multiple geometries 45, 46
  polygons 46, 47
  URL 42

[158]

GeoJSON data, choropleth map
  adding 70
  styling 71, 72
GeoJSON layers
  styling 48-50
GeoJSON, Leaflet.js
  as variable 43, 44
  data subset, displaying with filter 52
  iterating, through features 50
  marker, converting to GeoJSON layer 48
  pointToLayer option, using 51, 52
  pop ups, attaching with onEachFeature 50
GNU Image Manipulation Program (GIMP)
  about 78
  URL, for downloading 78
  used, for creating image for custom marker 78
gradient option, heatmap
  changing 60
graffiti layer
  querying 122, 123
group layers
  about 28
  feature group 30
  layer group 28, 29

H

HAML
  URL 137
heatmap
  about 55
  animating 67, 69
  creating 56
  creating, with esri-leaflet plugin 115, 116
  creating, with heatmap.js 62-65
  creating, with Leaflet.heat 56, 57
  data, adding 64
  density map 55
  intensity map 55
  markers, adding 61
  options, modifying 64
  styling, options 57
heatmap.js
  URL 62
  used, for creating heatmap 62-65

heatmap, styling
  blur value, changing 58-60
  gradient option, changing 60
  maxZoom option, changing 60
  radius value, changing 60
hosted copy
  used, for environment setup 8
HTML
  used, for mobile mapping 32-34

I

intensity map 55
interactive heatmap
  creating 65, 66

J

Jade, Node.js
  installing 136
  URL 136, 137
JavaScript
  referencing 8
  used, for creating mobile map 34-36
JavaScript Object Notation (JSON) 41
JavaScript plugin
  URL, for download 56

L

layer group 28, 29
Leaflet.js
  Leaflet.css file 9
  Leaflet file 9
  Leaflet-src.js file 9
  URL 9
Leaflet
  about 7
  addresses, geocoding 117
  choropleth map, creating with 69
  custom marker, creating in 82, 83
  esri-leaflet plugin, used for creating heatmap 115, 116
  querying with 153-155
  shapefile, using 110-113
  spatial queries, accessing 142-145
  URL 7

[159]

used, for creating basemap 8
used, for creating desktop application in C# 146
Leaflet.AnimatedMarker plugin
  autoStart option 98
  distance option 98
  interval option 98
  markers, animating with 96-100
  onEnd option 98
  URL, for downloading 96
Leaflet applications
  building, with CherryPy 138-142
  building, with Node.js 128
  building, with Python 138-142
Leaflet applications, building with Node.js
  AJAX calls, making 130-133
  Connect, using 134, 135
  Express, using 136-138
  Jade module, using 136
  Node.js server, creating 129, 130
Leaflet.BounceMarker plugin
  markers, animating with 95, 96
  URL, for downloading 95
Leaflet Data Visualization Framework
  about 100
  bar chart markers, creating with 103-105
  basic markers, creating 101, 102
  pie chart markers, creating with 103-105
  URL, for downloading 100
  using 100
Leaflet.heat
  options 57
  used, for creating heatmap 56, 57
Leaflet.heat methods
  about 60
  addLatLng() method 61
  redraw() method 61
  setLatLngs() method 61
  setOptions(options) 61
Leaflet.markercluster
  markers, clustering with 90
  URL 90
leaflet-shpfile plugin 111
L.Icon class
  about 82
  className option 82
  defining 84, 85
  iconAnchor option 82
  iconRetinaUrl option 82
  iconSize option 82
  iconUrl option 82
  popupAnchor option 82
  shadowAnchor option 82
  shadowRetinaUrl option 82
  shadowSize option 82
  shadowUrl option 82
local copy
  used, for environment setup 9

M

Maki markers
  URL, for downloading 86
  using 86, 87
map
  adding, to C# application 146-148
MapMarker, basic markers
  innerRadius option 102
  numberOfSides option 102
  radius option 102
  rotation option 102
map object, basemap
  creating 10
markercluster layer, options
  animateAddingMarkers 94, 95
  maxClusterRadius 94, 95
  removeOutsideVisibleBounds 93
  showCoverageOnHover 93
  spiderfyOnMaxZoom 93
  zoomToBoundsOnClick 93
markers
  adding, to C# application 149-151
  adding, to heatmap 61
  animating 95
  animating, with Leaflet.AnimatedMarker plugin 96-100
  animating, with Leaflet.BounceMarker plugin 95, 96
  creating 19
  clustering, with Leaflet.markercluster plugin 90
  cluster map, coding 90-92
  markercluster layer 93
  options 20

maxZoom option, heatmap
  changing 60
mobile map
  creating, with JavaScript 34-36
mobile mapping
  about 32
  CSS, using 32-34
  HTML, using 32-34
  with Leaflet map 32
MongoDB
  querying with 153-155
  spatial queries, accessing 142-145
  URL 139
  using, with C# and Leaflet 151-153
  using, with Python 139
multiple geometries, GeoJSON
  about 45, 46
  polygons 46, 47
multiple tile layers
  adding 16-18
  RAS_RIDGE_NEXRAD layer 17
MultiPolygons
  about 25
  creating 27
MultiPolylines
  about 25
  creating 26
Multivariate Kernel Density Estimation
  URL 56

N

National Oceanic and Atmospheric
    Administration. *See* NOAA
National Weather Service (NWS) 16
nearby() method 125
NOAA
  URL 17
Node.js
  Leaflet applications 128
  URL 128
  used, for building Leaflet applications 128
Node.js server
  creating, with Leaflet 129, 130
normalized choropleth map
  creating 73-75

O

onEachFeature option 50
Open Geospatial Consortium (OGC)
  about 15
  URL 15
OpenStreetMap tiles
  URL 11

P

pie chart markers
  creating, with Leaflet Data Visualization
      Framework 103-105
point
  adding, to basemap 19, 20
  addresses, geocoding to 117-119
  using, to find addresses 121
pointToLayer option 51, 52
polygons
  adding, to basemap 22
polylines
  adding, to basemap 21
pop up
  about 31, 32
  attaching, from onEachFeature option 50, 51
predefined markers
  Font Awesome markers, using 88, 89
  Maki markers, using 86, 87
  Twitter Bootstrap markers, using 88, 89
  using 86
projection file (.prj), shapefile 110
proximity query
  creating 124-126
Python
  spatial queries, accessing 143-145
  URL 138
  used, for building Leaflet
      applications 138-142

R

radius value, heatmap
  changing 60
rectangle
  about 23
  creating 23

redraw() method, Leaflet.heat 61
RegularPolygonMarker, basic markers
  innerRadius option 103
  numberOfSides option 103
  radius option 103
  rotation option 103
removeLayer() function 29
reverse geocoding
  about 121
  point, using 121

S

setLatLngs() method 61
setStyle() method 30, 49
shapefile
  about 110
  using, in Leaflet 110-113
spatial queries
  accessing, with Leaflet 142-145
  accessing, with MongoDB 142-145
  accessing, with Python 143-145
Stamen
  about 14
  tile layers 13
  URL 14
  URL, for creating maps 14
StarMarker, basic markers
  innerRadius option 103
  numberOfPoints option 103
  radius option 103
  rotation option 103
subset of data
  displaying, with filter 52

T

Thunderforest
  tile services 12
  using 13
tile layer
  adding 10, 11
  providers 12
tile layer providers
  Stamen 13
  Thunderforest 12
toGeoJson() method 48
toString() method 36
Twitter Bootstrap markers
  using 88, 89

U

United States Geological Survey (USGS) 15
URL parameters
  geocoding 119, 120

W

Web Mapping Service (WMS)
  about 15
  URL 15
WMS tile layer
  adding 15, 16

Thank you for buying
Leaflet.js Essentials

About Packt Publishing

Packt, pronounced 'packed', published its first book "*Mastering phpMyAdmin for Effective MySQL Management*" in April 2004 and subsequently continued to specialize in publishing highly focused books on specific technologies and solutions.

Our books and publications share the experiences of your fellow IT professionals in adapting and customizing today's systems, applications, and frameworks. Our solution based books give you the knowledge and power to customize the software and technologies you're using to get the job done. Packt books are more specific and less general than the IT books you have seen in the past. Our unique business model allows us to bring you more focused information, giving you more of what you need to know, and less of what you don't.

Packt is a modern, yet unique publishing company, which focuses on producing quality, cutting-edge books for communities of developers, administrators, and newbies alike. For more information, please visit our website: `www.packtpub.com`.

About Packt Open Source

In 2010, Packt launched two new brands, Packt Open Source and Packt Enterprise, in order to continue its focus on specialization. This book is part of the Packt Open Source brand, home to books published on software built around Open Source licenses, and offering information to anybody from advanced developers to budding web designers. The Open Source brand also runs Packt's Open Source Royalty Scheme, by which Packt gives a royalty to each Open Source project about whose software a book is sold.

Writing for Packt

We welcome all inquiries from people who are interested in authoring. Book proposals should be sent to `author@packtpub.com`. If your book idea is still at an early stage and you would like to discuss it first before writing a formal book proposal, contact us; one of our commissioning editors will get in touch with you.

We're not just looking for published authors; if you have strong technical skills but no writing experience, our experienced editors can help you develop a writing career, or simply get some additional reward for your expertise.

[PACKT] open source
community experience distilled
PUBLISHING

Instant Interactive Map designs with Leaflet JavaScript Library How-to

ISBN: 978-1-78216-520-0　　　　Paperback: 52 pages

An intuitive guide to creating animated, interactive maps with the Leaflet JavaScript library in a series of straightforward recipes

1. Learn something new in an Instant! A short, fast, focused guide delivering immediate results.
2. Create user-friendly, interactive maps for desktop and mobile platforms.
3. Deploy maps for desktop and mobile platforms.

Google Maps JavaScript API Cookbook

ISBN: 978-1-84969-882-5　　　　Paperback: 316 pages

Over 50 recipes to help you create web maps and GIS web applications using the Google Maps JavaScript API

1. Add to your website's functionality by utilizing Google Maps' power.
2. Full of code examples and screenshots for practical and efficient learning.
3. Empowers you to build your own mapping application from the ground up.

Please check **www.PacktPub.com** for information on our titles

Optimizing Hadoop for MapReduce

ISBN: 978-1-78328-565-5   Paperback: 120 pages

Learn how to configure your Hadoop cluster to run optimal MapReduce jobs

1. Optimize your MapReduce job performance.
2. Identify your Hadoop cluster's weaknesses.
3. Tune your MapReduce configuration.

PostGIS Cookbook

ISBN: 978-1-84951-866-6   Paperback: 484 pages

Over 80 task-based recipes to store, organize, manipulate, and analyze spatial data in a PostGIS database

1. Integrate PostGIS with web frameworks and implement OGC standards such as WMS and WFS using MapServer and GeoServer.
2. Convert 2D and 3D vector data, raster data, and routing data into usable forms.
3. Visualize data from the PostGIS database using a desktop GIS program such as QGIS and OpenJUMP.
4. Easy-to-use recipes with advanced analyses of spatial data and practical applications.

Please check **www.PacktPub.com** for information on our titles

Printed in Great Britain
by Amazon.co.uk, Ltd.,
Marston Gate.